Editor **NICK PULFORD**

**Designed by David Dew**

Cover designed by Duncan Olner

## Contributors

| | | |
|---|---|---|
| Richard Birch | David Jennings | Craig Thake |
| Mark Brown | Kevin Morley | Nick Watts |
| Scott Burton | Graeme Rodway | Richard Young |
| Matt Gardner | Stefan Searle | |
| Jack Haynes | Tom Segal | |

**With grateful thanks to Ascot Racecourse for their invaluable assistance**

Published in 2023 by Pitch Publishing on behalf of Racing Post, 9 Donnington Park, 85 Birdham Road, Chichester, West Sussex PO20 7AJ. www.pitchpublishing.co.uk info@pitchpublishing.co.uk

Pitch Publishing specifies that post-press changes may occur to any information given in this publication. A catalogue record for this book is available from the British Library.

ISBN 978-1-83950-142-5
Printed in Great Britain by Pure Print

8

48

94

108

186

## Editor Nick Pulford looks forward to Royal Ascot 2023

*R*oyal Ascot is always a special occasion, but in Coronation year it will be just a little different. The new king is on the throne and there will be enormous interest in the handover of one of the great traditions of the royal calendar.

The 2023 meeting falls just over six weeks after the coronation and will be one of the first joint-engagements for King Charles and Queen Camilla. The eyes of the world will be watching when they lead their first royal procession down the straight mile and take their places in the famous Royal Enclosure to watch the afternoon's sport.

It is one of the occasions when we have become used to seeing the royal family at their most relaxed. There are formalities to the dress and protocols, but there is also a great sense of fun and enjoyment. A royal runner or two only adds to the excitement.

The people will come from every corner of the realm, some arriving by Rolls-Royce or helicopter, many in packed trains and on coach parties. Friends and families will get together. There will be picnics in the car parks and on the lawns. Champagne and caviar. Colourful fashion from the classic to the outlandish. Chatter and cheering, smiles and singing.

Just like the vast crowds, the racecourse will be dressed to impress. It is a special place to be in June.

The racing is something else. Based on Racing Post Ratings, 14 of the top 25 performers in Britain and Ireland last year ran at Royal Ascot, headed by the brilliant Baaeed. Their number was boosted by top Australian sprinter Nature Strip.

Eight Group 1 races pepper the week, starting with the rapid burst of the Queen Anne, King's Stand and St James's Palace Stakes inside the opening two hours. Heritage handicaps, high-class two-year-old races and great staying contests add even more competition and variety.

Thirty-five races are now the norm and they present a remarkable concentration of quality in five days of racing. Each day has something special. Put them all together and you have the most magical week.

5

# ROYAL ASCOT ESSENTIALS

## DATES

- Royal Ascot 2023 takes place over five days from Tuesday June 20 to Saturday June 24

## TICKETS

- **Royal Enclosure** Available only to members and their guests, or non-members with a hospitality guest day badge
- **Queen Anne Enclosure** £90 Tue & Wed, £99 Thu-Sat
- **Village Enclosure** £85 Thu-Sat
- **Windsor Enclosure** £49 Tue & Wed, £65 Thu, £69 Fri & Sat
- For more details, see pages 8-15

## BY CAR

- **From London & the North** M4 Junction 6 onto the A332 Windsor bypass and follow the signs to Ascot
- **From the West** M4 Junction 10 to the A329(M) signed to Bracknell and follow the signs to Ascot
- **From the South & East** M3 Junction 3 onto the A332 signed to Bracknell and follow the signs to Ascot
- **From the Midlands** M40 southbound, Junction 4. Take the A404 towards the M4 (Junction 8/9). On the M4 head towards Heathrow/London. Leave M4 at Junction 6 and follow the A332 Windsor bypass to Ascot
- More than 8,000 car parking spaces are available and pre-booking is advised. Car Park 8 costs £40 per day

## BY TRAIN

- South Western Railway runs a frequent service to Ascot from Reading, Guildford and London Waterloo. The average journey time is 27 minutes from Reading and 52 minutes from Waterloo. The railway station is a seven-minute walk from the racecourse

## TV DETAILS

- All 35 races will be broadcast live on ITV, with 30 hours of live coverage across the week. The Opening Show preview programme will be shown daily at 9am on ITV4 and coverage of the racing will start at 1.30pm
- Sky Sports Racing will also broadcast live from Ascot on each of the five days

# THE ENCLOSURES

From the Royal Enclosure and its strict dress code to
the more relaxed Windsor Enclosure, Ascot has four
distinct areas to suit different pockets and tastes

# ROYAL ENCLOSURE

**Where is it?** This is the most exclusive area with the best views from the grandstand and by the winning post. Members have access to Level 4 of the grandstand and the Royal Enclosure Gardens.

**How much does it cost?** Membership is by invitation only. Members can book badges for themselves and their guests, and non-members can gain access with a hospitality guest day badge.

**What's the vibe?** There is a sense of formality and decorum but plenty to enjoy for racing and fashion watchers from the best seats in the house.

**What's the dress code?** Men are required to wear black, grey or navy morning dress which must include a waistcoat and tie, a black or grey top hat and black shoes. Women must wear formal daywear with a hat and the various rules include: dresses and skirts should be of modest length defined as falling just above the knee or longer; dresses and tops should have straps of one inch or greater.

**Hang out at** the Mill Reef Bar. Named after the famous 1970 Coventry Stakes winner, this bar is located in a quiet area near the entrance from Car Park 1.

**Do it in style at** the Parade Ring Restaurant, located on Level 2 of the grandstand and regarded as the jewel in the crown for fine dining at Ascot. Three Michelin-starred chef Simon Rogan takes the helm this year. Prices from £2,099pp.

# QUEEN ANNE ENCLOSURE

**Where is it?** This is the premier public enclosure right at the heart of the action, offering access to the parade ring, pre-parade and ground floor of the grandstand. Guests can see the horses before and after each race and there are excellent views of the racing and royal procession from the trackside lawns and grandstand viewing steps.

**How much does it cost?** Advance tickets are £90 for Tuesday and Wednesday, rising to £99 for Thursday, Friday and Saturday.

**What's the vibe?** While there is a strict dress code, there is the feel of an English garden party with plenty to interest racing aficionados and occasional racegoers alike. One of the highlights is the communal singing at the bandstand in the heart of the enclosure after racing each day.

**What's the dress code?** Guests are required to dress for a formal daytime occasion. Men must wear a full-length suit (with jacket and trousers of matching material) with a collared shirt and tie. Women must wear a hat, headpiece or fascinator at all times. Strapless and sheer dresses and tops are not permitted; nor are jeans or trainers.

**Food and drink** A wide range is on offer from street food to elegant walk-up restaurants. Highlights include champagne bars by Moët & Chandon, the 1768 Grill and Tea Rooms and popular on-the-go eateries such as Baos At The Bandstand and Sussex Charmer Cheese On Toast.

**Eat at** The Bandstand Kitchen & Bar with its wide range from Ascot brunch to bar snacks and pastries. Located in the heart of the action at the rear of the grandstand with outdoor seating.

**Hang out at** the Stewards' House Cocktail Bar, which serves a classic selection and has a relaxed feel with a lawned area looking down over the bandstand.

**Do it in style at** The Gallery. With a first-floor view of the track and a private balcony, this restaurant offers formal yet relaxed dining with a three-course luncheon menu from £549pp.

# THE ENCLOSURES

# VILLAGE ENCLOSURE

**Where is it?** The Village Enclosure is located in the centre of the track, looking back towards the grandstand from the other side of the rails, and offers a different view of the racing as the horses thunder down the home straight.

**How much does it cost?** The Village Enclosure is open only on the last three days and advance tickets are £85 per day.

**What's the vibe?** Described by Ascot as "relaxed and vibrant", the newest of Royal Ascot's enclosures is aimed at a younger crowd, featuring DJs and a range of live music. The party goes on for almost three hours after racing until 9pm.

**What's the dress code?** Less formal than that of the Queen Anne Enclosure but guests are asked to dress for a formal daytime occasion. Men are required to wear full-length trousers or chinos and a suit jacket or blazer with a collared shirt and tie, while women must wear a hat, headpiece or fascinator at all times. Strapless and sheer dresses and tops are not permitted; nor are jeans or trainers.

**Food and drink** The relaxed atmosphere is reflected in a range of on-the-go food options, from artisanal ice-creams to Indian and Japanese street food, along with champagne and cocktail bars.

**Eat at** Babek Brothers for gourmet kebabs with ingredients sourced from Devon farms. In a covered seating area and also serving a selection of cocktails.

**Hang out at** Village Green Bar. Close to the action with good views and serving wines, spirits, craft beers and champagne, along with the Plymouth Fruit Cup and Royal Ascot Blush.

**Do it in style at** The Villiers Club. Guests enjoy a two-course meal and afternoon tea along with complimentary beer, wine and soft drinks, plus live DJ and bands within the marquee and private garden throughout the day. From £299 per person.

# WINDSOR ENCLOSURE

**Where is it?** This area is located furthest up the course from the winning post.

**How much does it cost?** Advance tickets are £49 for Tuesday and Wednesday, rising to £65 for Thursday and £69 for Friday and Saturday.

**What's the vibe?** This is the least formal of the four enclosures, offering a relaxed day at the races with picnics on the lawns complemented by a range of bars and eating outlets serving British classics such as fish and chips, along with ice cream, burgers, hot dogs and street food.

**What's the dress code?** There are no official rules but guests are encouraged to dress in smart daywear. It is recommended that men wear a jacket, collared shirt and full-length trousers and women dress in smart attire with a hat or fascinator.

**Hang out at** the lawns. Bring a picnic and a bottle of fizz and find a space on the extensive grassed area to settle in for the day.

**Do it in style with** a picnic. Pre-book a Best of British Picnic at £95 for two people to share. Sample menu: hot smoked salmon pate (starter), chicken salad (main), espresso martini mousse (dessert), plus cheese and crackers.

| | | | |
|---|---|---|---|
| **2.30 Queen Anne Stakes** (Group 1)<br>Last year's winner: Baaeed 1-6f | **1m** 4yo+ | | £750,000 |
| **3.05 Coventry Stakes** (Group 2)<br>Last year's winner: Bradsell 8-1 | **6f** 2yo | | £150,000 |
| **3.40 King's Stand Stakes** (Group 1)<br>Last year's winner: Nature Strip 9-4 | **5f** 3yo+ | | £600,000 |
| **4.20 St James's Palace Stakes** (Group 1)<br>Last year's winner: Coroebus 10-11f | **1m** 3yo colts | | £600,000 |
| **5.00 Ascot Stakes** (Handicap)<br>Last year's winner: Coltrane 14-1 | **2m4f** 4yo+ | | £100,000 |
| **5.35 Wolferton Stakes** (Listed)<br>Last year's winner: Dubai Future 20-1 | **1m2f** 4yo+ | | £110,000 |
| **6.10 Copper Horse Stakes** (Handicap)<br>Last year's winner: Get Shirty 16-1 | **1m6f** 4yo+ | | £100,000 |

Race value is total prize-money

ROYAL ASCOT goes big from the start with a blockbuster Tuesday featuring three Group 1 showpiece events in a breathless opening couple of hours.

First out of the gates is the Queen Anne Stakes down the straight course for the older elite milers. The historic contest is a major stepping stone to championship honours and never more so than last year when top-class winner Baaeed recorded a Racing Post Rating of 131 on his way to the Horse of the Year title.

Not far behind him on last year's Royal Ascot honours list was Australian speedster Nature Strip in the King's Stand Stakes, the second top-level race on the card. His RPR of 129 marked him out as the sprinter of the year and arguably the best of the seven raiders from outside Europe to have landed the King's Stand since it took on a truly international flavour 20 years ago.

The third Group 1 of the day is the St James's Palace Stakes, which brings together the top three-year-old milers for a showdown on the round course. Last year's race went to Coroebus, doubling up after his 2,000 Guineas success, and another clash between the Guineas principals from around Europe will be hotly anticipated.

The supporting cast includes the Group 2

# ROYAL ASCOT

Coventry Stakes, renowned as the premier race for two-year-old colts at the meeting and often the first showcase for a top-class performer. All of last year's first four ranked in the top 12 juveniles of 2022 on RPRs.

The day's main handicap is the Ascot Stakes over the marathon trip of two and a half miles. This has become a major target for the top jumps trainers as well as the big Flat stables, with Irish champion jumps trainer Willie Mullins the strongest force in recent years.

Next comes the Wolferton Stakes, a Listed race over a mile and a quarter for four-year-olds and upwards, while staying handicappers also round off the day in the Copper Horse Stakes over a mile and three-quarters.

# DAY ONE

FIRST run in 1840, the Queen Anne Stakes commemorates the monarch who established racing at Ascot and is the meeting's top mile race for older horses (aged four and up).

## Last year's winner

Baaeed, at odds of 1-6, was head and shoulders above his rivals and scored by a length and three-quarters. He fitted every key trend.

**Form** Eight of the last ten winners came into the race with an adjusted Racing Post Rating of at least 132 and seven already had Group 1 success on their record. The two who did not fit either pattern were Declaration Of War (2013) and Accidental Agent (2018), although both had run in a Group 1 last time (fifth and sixth in the Lockinge).

**Key races** The Lockinge is the main stepping stone – the last 11 British-trained winners of the Queen Anne had run in the Newbury Group 1 (finishing 82411116011). Two of Aidan O'Brien's last three winners also prepped in the Lockinge (finishing 65) and the US-based Tepin in 2016 is the only one of the last 16 winners who had not run at the top level last time (a Grade 2 at Churchill Downs in her case) – the three French-trained winners had all run in the Prix d'Ispahan.

Often the previous year's Guineas and Royal Ascot results are a good sign of the right quality. Nine of the 17 four-year-old winners since 2000 had secured a top-three finish in a Guineas (three won) or in the St James's Palace Stakes (four won). Most of the other four-year-old winners were late developers or had been held up by injury the previous year.

## Story of the last ten years

| | FORM | WINNER | AGE & WGT | Adj RPR | SP | TRAINER | BEST RPR LAST 12 MONTHS (RUNS SINCE) |
|---|---|---|---|---|---|---|---|
| 22 | 111-1 | **Baaeed** CD | 4 9-2 | 141ᵀ | 1-6f | William Haggas | won Lockinge Stakes Gp1 (1m) (0) |
| 21 | 13-11 | **Palace Pier** C, D | 4 9-0 | 141ᵀ | 2-7f | John & Thady Gosden | won Lockinge Stakes Gp1 (1m) (0) |
| 20 | 2714- | **Circus Maximus** C. D, BF | 4 9-0 | 133-3 | 4-1f | Aidan O'Brien (IRE) | won Prix du Moulin Gp1 (1m) (1) |
| 19 | 66-30 | **Lord Glitters** CD | 6 9-0 | 132-4 | 14-1 | David O'Meara | 3rd Dubai Turf Gp1 (1m1f) (1) |
| 18 | 48-36 | **Accidental Agent** C | 4 9-0 | 127-10 | 33-1 | Eve Johnson Houghton | won Ascot Class 2 handicap (7f) (4) |
| 17 | 12-31 | **Ribchester** C, D | 4 9-0 | 139ᵀ | 11-10f | Richard Fahey | won Lockinge Stakes Gp1 (1m) (0) |
| 16 | -1111 | **Tepin** D | 5 8-11 | 138ᵀ | 11-2 | Mark Casse (CAN) | won Keeneland Gd1 (1m½f) (1) |
| 15 | 1-111 | **Solow** D | 5 9-0 | 139-2 | 11-8f | Freddy Head (FR) | won Dubai Turf Gp1 (1m1f) (1) |
| 14 | 4216- | **Toronado** C, D | 4 9-0 | 143ᵀ | 4-5f | Richard Hannon | won Sussex Stakes Gp1 (1m) (1) |
| 13 | 11-15 | **Declaration Of War** D, BF | 4 9-0 | 128-11 | 15-2 | Aidan O'Brien (IRE) | won Leopardstown Listed (1m) (1) |

**WINS-PL-RUNS** 4yo 7-10-54, 5yo 2-7-39, 6yo+ 1-2-31 **FAVOURITES** £3.73

**TRAINERS IN THIS RACE** (w-pl-r) Aidan O'Brien 2-4-13, Richard Hannon 1-0-10, John & Thady Gosden 1-0-1, William Haggas 1-2-4, Andrew Balding 0-1-6, Roger Varian 0-2-8, Saeed bin Suroor 0-1-3, Charlie Appleby 0-0-2, Charlie Hills 0-0-3

**FATE OF FAVOURITES** 0112100111 **POSITION OF WINNER IN MARKET** 2113106111

Baaeed stamps his authority on last year's Queen Anne with the performance of the meeting

## Key trends
▶*Aged four or five, nine winners in last ten runnings*
▶*Distance winner, 9/10*
▶*Rated within 4lb of RPR top-rated, 8/10 (five were top-rated)*
▶*Adjusted Racing Post Rating of at least 132, 8/10*
▶*Group 1 winner, 7/10*

## Other factors
▶*Seven winners had previously scored at the track*

## Roll of honour
**Longest-priced winner**
Garrick 50-1 (1950)

**Shortest-priced winner**
Frankel 1-10 (2012)

**Most successful trainer**
7 wins: **Saeed bin Suroor**
Charnwood Forest (1996), Allied Forces (1997), Intikhab (1998), Cape Cross (1999), Dubai Destination (2003), Refuse To Bend (2004), Ramonti (2007)

**Most successful jockey**
7 wins: **Frankie Dettori**
Markofdistinction (1990), Allied Forces (1997), Intikhab (1998), Dubai Destination (2003), Refuse To Bend (2004), Ramonti (2007), Palace Pier (2021)

**Most successful owner**
8 wins: **Godolphin**
Charnwood Forest (1996), Allied Forces (1997), Intikhab (1998), Cape Cross (1999), Dubai Destination (2003), Refuse To Bend (2004), Ramonti (2007), Ribchester (2017)

*All figures since 1946

**Trainers** Two yards to note are Ballydoyle and the Hannon stable. Since 2008 with fancied runners (below 10-1) the form figures for O'Brien (*right*) are 1662129518 and for the Hannons they are 121154. The recent French record is good, with three wins and five places from 18 runners since 2005.

**Betting** Baaeed was the eighth successful favourite in the last 12 runnings and the third in a row. That marks a resumption of the normal pattern following a couple of upsets for Accidental Agent (33-1) and Lord Glitters (14-1) in 2018 and 2019. Before them, the last winner from outside the top four in the betting was Refuse To Bend (12-1) in 2004.

# 3.05 Coventry Stakes

FIRST run in 1890, this is the most valuable race for juveniles at Royal Ascot and the season's first high-class contest for the age group, regularly proving a stepping stone to Group 1 level later in the year.

## Last year's winner

Bradsell fitted several key trends – being once-racedand a distance winner by at least two lengths. The placed horses, Persian Force and Royal Scotsman, had run twice. All were last-time-out winners.

**Form** One run is often enough to prepare for this test, as it was for 11 winners in the past 20 years (only three winners in that period had run more than twice). All but one of those once-raced juveniles had won, and indeed just five of the last 20 winners had suffered a defeat before

## Key trends

▶ *Won last time out, 9/10*
▶ *No more than three starts, 9/10*
▶ *Won a previous start by at least two lengths, 7/10*
▶ *Rated within 7lb of RPR top-rated, 6/10 (exceptions 12lb to 22lb off top)*
▶ *Adjusted RPR of at least 110, 6/10*
▶ *Distance winner, 6/10*

## Other factors

▶ *Seven winners were undefeated. Buratino, who won in 2015, had been beaten twice over 5f but was undefeated over 6f*
▶ *The market is usually a strong indicator but four winners since 2013 were priced in at least double figures*

Ascot. The only winner this century to arrive off the back of a last-time-out defeat was

150-1 shot Nando Parrado in 2020.

**Key races** Southern-trained contenders often start in a Newmarket or Newbury maiden/novice; York is a good route for a northern challenger; in Ireland, check the Curragh and Leopardstown. Three of the last ten winners made their debut on the all-weather. Only one of the last ten winners had competed in Pattern company (winning the Listed Marble Hill Stakes at the Curragh).

**Trainers** Aidan O'Brien is the top trainer with nine victories since his first with Harbour Master in 1997 (six of the nine were favourite).

**Betting** Market position is a good guide, with 16 of the last 20 winners having been in the first four in the betting and only four of those 20 priced above 8-1.

## Story of the last ten years

| FORM | WINNER | AGE & WGT | Adj RPR | SP | TRAINER | BEST RPR LAST 12 MONTHS (RUNS SINCE) |
|------|--------|-----------|---------|-----|---------|--------------------------------------|
| 22 1 | **Bradsell** D | 2 9-3 | 111-7 | 8-1 | Archie Watson | won York Class 3 novice (6f) (0) |
| 21 1 | **Berkshire Shadow** | 2 9-1 | 102-14 | 11-1 | Andrew Balding | won Newbury Class 4 maiden (5f) (0) |
| 20 5 | **Nando Parrado** | 2 9-1 | 81-22 | 150-1 | Clive Cox | 5th Newmarket Class 5 maiden (6f) (0) |
| 19 21 | **Arizona** D | 2 9-1 | 111T | 15-8f | Aidan O'Brien (IRE) | won Curragh maiden (6f) (0) |
| 18 1 | **Calyx** D | 2 9-1 | 115-2 | 2-1f | John Gosden | won Newmarket Class 4 novice (6f) (0) |
| 17 1 | **Rajasinghe** D | 2 9-1 | 103-13 | 11-1 | Richard Spencer | won Newcastle Class 4 novice (6f) (0) |
| 16 11 | **Caravaggio** | 2 9-1 | 119T | 13-8f | Aidan O'Brien (IRE) | won Marble Hill Stakes Listed (5f) (0) |
| 15 13121 | **Buratino** D | 2 9-1 | 118T | 6-1 | Mark Johnston | won Woodcote Stakes Listed (6f) (0) |
| 14 1 | **The Wow Signal** D | 2 9-1 | 110-4 | 5-1j | John Quinn | won Ayr Class 4 maiden (6f) (0) |
| 13 1 | **War Command** D | 2 9-1 | 104-12 | 20-1 | Aidan O'Brien (IRE) | won Leopardstown maiden (7f) (0) |

**FAVOURITES** £1.50 **TRAINERS IN THIS RACE** (w-pl-r) Aidan O'Brien 3-4-18, Archie Watson 1-1-4, Andrew Balding 1-0-2, Clive Cox 1-0-7, Jim Bolger 0-0-1, Charlie Appleby 0-0-5, Richard Hannon 0-4-13, Wesley Ward 0-0-3, John & Thady Gosden 0-0-2

**FATE OF FAVOURITES** 6101411064 **POSITION OF WINNER IN MARKET** 9131611064

# Summer has arrived at
## Nirvana Spa

Spa visits from £60

Scan to discover

# DAY ONE

IRST run in 1860, this five-furlong contest is the fastest race of the week, usually completed in less than a minute. Having been a Group 2 for 20 years, the race regained Group 1 status in 2008.

**Last year's winner** Nature Strip fitted all the key trends including a higher-numbered draw (stall ten in the 16-runner-field). He was a throwback to Australia's dominance of the noughties (four winners in seven runnings from 2003 to 2009), since when the non-European winners had been from Hong Kong (Little Bridge in 2012) and USA (Lady Aurelia in 2017).

**Form** Group 1-winning form is important with overseas raiders (all five Australian winners and Lady Aurelia qualified, with Hong Kong's Little Bridge an exception) but not so much for the British and Irish (four of the last ten were scoring for the first time at this level). A good level of Group form is virtually a must, however.

Four of the last ten winners were top on adjusted Racing Post Ratings and no winner in the past decade was more than 7lb off top (that measure narrowed the field from 16 to four last year).

## Story of the last ten years

| FORM | | WINNER | AGE & WGT | Adj RPR | SP | TRAINER | BEST RPR LAST 12 MONTHS (RUNS SINCE) |
|---|---|---|---|---|---|---|---|
| 22 | 1-231 | **Nature Strip** D | 7 9-5 | 133$^T$ | 9-4 | Chris Waller (AUS) | won TJ Smith Stakes Gp1 (6f) (0) |
| 21 | 5-723 | **Oxted** BF | 5 9-5 | 129$^{-3}$ | 4-1 | Roger Teal | won July Cup Gp1 (6f) (4) |
| 20 | 2110- | **Battaash** D, BF | 6 9-4 | 139$^T$ | 5-6f | Charlie Hills | won Nunthorpe Stakes Gp1 (5f) (1) |
| 19 | 3-111 | **Blue Point** CD | 5 9-4 | 133$^{-6}$ | 5-2 | Charlie Appleby | won Al Quoz Sprint Gp1 (6f) (0) |
| 18 | 41-29 | **Blue Point** C | 4 9-4 | 131$^{-7}$ | 6-1 | Charlie Appleby | 2nd Meydan Gp2 (5f) (1) |
| 17 | 113-1 | **Lady Aurelia** CD | 3 8-9 | 138$^T$ | 7-2 | Wesley Ward (USA) | won Keeneland Listed (5½f) (0) |
| 16 | 05-11 | **Profitable** D | 4 9-4 | 131$^{-3}$ | 4-1 | Clive Cox | won Temple Stakes Gp2 (5f) (0) |
| 15 | 42-17 | **Goldream** CD | 6 9-4 | 125$^{-6}$ | 20-1 | Robert Cowell | won Palace House Stakes Gp3 (5f) (1) |
| 14 | 2-471 | **Sole Power** CD | 7 9-4 | 130$^T$ | 5-1 | Eddie Lynam (IRE) | won King's Stand Stakes Gp1 (5f) (7) |
| 13 | -2414 | **Sole Power** D, BF | 6 9-4 | 127$^{-6}$ | 8-1 | Eddie Lynam (IRE) | won Palace House Stakes Gp3 (5f) (1) |

**WINS-PL-RUNS** 3yo 1-3-19, 4yo 2-8-49, 5yo 2-5-34, 6yo+ 5-4-54 **FAVOURITES** -£8.17

**TRAINERS IN THIS RACE** (w-pl-r) Charlie Appleby 2-0-6, Eddie Lynam 2-0-3, Wesley Ward 1-0-4, Roger Teal 1-0-1, Chris Waller 1-0-1, John Quinn 0-1-4, Aidan O'Brien 0-0-9, Tim Easterby 0-0-9, Roger Varian 0-0-4, Andrew Balding 0-0-3

**FATE OF FAVOURITES** 2350302140 **POSITION OF WINNER IN MARKET** 4382232122

# 3.40 King's Stand Stakes

**Key races** Six of the last ten winners from Britain and Ireland had contested the Palace House Stakes at Newmarket or the Temple Stakes at Haydock (and frequently both) that season and five of them had won at least one of those contests (the other was third) – a win in the Palace House seems to count for more, with five of the last nine to attempt the double being successful (compared with only one of the last 12 Temple winners to try).

Significant races from further afield are the Prix du Gros-Chene (The Tatling in 2004, Equiano in 2008 and Prohibit in 2011 all placed before coming here) and the Prix de Saint-Georges, won by French-trained Chineur before his King's Stand victory in 2005 (Prohibit fourth in 2011).

**Trainers** As well as top-level international trainers, the roll of honour includes several noted for their handling of sprinters – Robert Cowell (Prohibit in 2011 and Goldream in 2015), Eddie Lynam (Sole Power in 2013 and 2014) and Clive Cox (Profitable in 2016).

**Betting** Favourites can be found out (only three of the last 28 have won and last year Golden Pal was last at 15-8) but the market is still a good guide. Since Choisir's 25-1 breakthrough success for Australia in 2003, at a time when the strength of their challenge was underestimated, 16 of the 19 winners have been no bigger than 8-1.

## Key trends
▸ *Adjusted RPR of at least 125, 10/10*
▸ *Rated within 7lb of RPR top-rated, 10/10*
▸ *Ran at least twice that season, 8/10*
▸ *Drawn eight or higher, 8/10*
▸ *Group winner over 5f, 8/10*
▸ *Won that season, 7/10*

## Other factors
▸ *In 2020, Battaash became the first successful favourite since Scenic Blast in 2009*
▸ *Six beaten favourites had won a Group race last time*
▸ *The record of Palace House winners is 1111334*

## Roll of honour
**Longest-priced winners**
Squander Bug (1948) & Don't Worry Me (1997), 33-1

**Shortest-priced winner**
Lochsong 3-10 (1994)

**Most successful trainer**
5 wins: **Vincent O'Brien**
Cassarate (1952), Abergwaun (1973), Godswalk (1977), Solinus (1978), Bluebird (1987)

**Most successful jockey**
7 wins: **Lester Piggott**
Right Boy (1957), Majority Rule (1963), Swing Easy (1971), Abergwaun (1973), Godswalk (1977), Solinus (1978), Never So Bold (1985)

*All figures since 1946

# DAY ONE

FIRST run in 1834, this mile contest for three-year-old colts is the third Group 1 of the opening day and often features a clash between the Guineas combatants in Britain, France and Ireland.

## Last year's winner

Coroebus, having won the 2,000 Guineas, had the ideal profile and delivered at odds-on, albeit by just a head from 28-1 shot Lusail (who had been sixth at Newmarket).

**Form** Guineas form is key. Coroebus was the 20th winner in the last 24 runnings to have run in at least one Guineas and he was the 15th of those 20 to have enjoyed Classic success (some had done so in more than one of them). Four more had been runner-up, with the worst position being Excellent Art's fourth in the French Guineas in 2007.

**Key races** Twelve of the last 23 winners had run in both the Newmarket and Irish Guineas and Poetic Flare in 2021 was only the third of those to go backwards on the second run in terms of their finishing position (Zafeen was 14th in Ireland after being runner-up at Newmarket in 2003 and Galileo Gold went from first to second in 2016). Of the seven who did not win at Newmarket, four stepped up to first place in Ireland.

Three of the last 13 winners – Canford Cliffs (2010), Kingman (2014) and Barney Roy (2017) – reversed form here after a Guineas defeat at Newmarket. The first two of those had preceded Ascot success with Guineas victory in Ireland, while Barney Roy had not run in between. Mastercraftsman in 2009 also reversed Newmarket form with the best performer from that Classic (winner Sea The Stars did not run at Ascot, having gone on to win the Derby instead).

**Trainers** Not surprisingly, given his tremendous strength in depth in the Classics division, Aidan O'Brien has won eight of the last 23 runnings. Between them, his eight winners had

run in 13 Guineas with form figures of 2261114115111 – five of them had won a Guineas and three had done the Newmarket/Irish Guineas double.

**Betting** The preponderance of strong Guineas form means favourites have a good record, with 14 winning in the 23 runnings since 2000. No winner has been bigger than 10-1 in that period and only one (Circus Maximus) came from outside the top four in the betting. The last shock winner was Brief Truce at 25-1 in 1992.

William Buick salutes the crowd after his victory with Coroebus in last year's St James's Palace

## Key trends
- From the first three in the market, 9/10
- Rated within 7lb of RPR top-rated, 8/10 (six were top-rated)
- Had won or placed in a Group 1, 7/10
- Adjusted RPR of at least 132, 7/10
- Had finished in the first three in a 2,000 Guineas, 7/10

## Other factors
- Winners who had run in a Guineas finished 1211211 at Newmarket and 1122 at the Curragh. The 2021

winner Poetic Flare also ran in the French Guineas (sixth) – the first since Excellent Art in 2007 (fourth)
- Four winners had run in the British and Irish Guineas, with all making the frame in both
- Without Parole in 2018 and Palace Pier in 2020 (both trained by John Gosden) are the only two winners not to have run in a Group 1 that season since Shavian in 1990
- Aidan O'Brien has won eight of the last 23 runnings

# 4.20 St James's Palace Stakes

## Story of the last ten years

| FORM | WINNER | AGE | & WGT | Adj RPR | SP | TRAINER | BEST RPR LAST 12 MONTHS (RUNS SINCE) |
|---|---|---|---|---|---|---|---|
| 22 | 121-1 **Coroebus** D | 3 | 9-2 | 135$^T$ | 10-11f | Charlie Appleby | won 2,000 Guineas Gp1 (1m) (0) |
| 21 | -1162 **Poetic Flare** D | 3 | 9-0 | 134$^T$ | 7-2f | Jim Bolger (IRE) | won 2,000 Guineas Gp1 (1m) (2) |
| 20 | 11-1 **Palace Pier** D | 3 | 9-0 | 127$^{-15}$ | 4-1 | John Gosden | won Newcastle Class 2 hcap (1m) (0) |
| 19 | 34-16 **Circus Maximus** D | 3 | 9-0 | 126$^{-13}$ | 10-1 | Aidan O'Brien (IRE) | 4th Futurity Trophy Gp1 (1m) (2) |
| 18 | 1-11 **Without Parole** D | 3 | 9-0 | 128$^{-7}$ | 9-4f | John Gosden | won Yarmouth Class 5 novice (1m) (1) |
| 17 | 1-12 **Barney Roy** C, D | 3 | 9-0 | 132$^{-7}$ | 5-2 | Richard Hannon | 2nd 2,000 Guineas Gp1 (1m) (0) |
| 16 | 13-12 **Galileo Gold** D, BF | 3 | 9-0 | 137$^T$ | 6-1 | Hugo Palmer | won 2,000 Guineas Gp1 (1m) (1) |
| 15 | 11d-11 **Gleneagles** D | 3 | 9-0 | 137$^T$ | 8-15f | Aidan O'Brien (IRE) | won 2,000 Guineas Gp1 (1m) (1) |
| 14 | 1-121 **Kingman** D | 3 | 9-0 | 140$^T$ | 8-11f | John Gosden | won Irish 2,000 Guineas Gp1 (1m) (0) |
| 13 | 11-10 **Dawn Approach** C, D, BF | 3 | 9-0 | 141$^T$ | 5-4f | Jim Bolger (IRE) | won 2,000 Guineas Gp1 (1m) (1) |

**FAVOURITES** £5.17 **TRAINERS IN THIS RACE (w-pl-r)** Aidan O'Brien 2-5-22, Richard Hannon 1-2-7, Hugo Palmer 1-0-2, Charlie Appleby 1-2-7, John & Thady Gosden 0-0-2, Andrew Balding 0-0-2, Richard Fahey 0-0-1

**FATE OF FAVOURITES** 1112413211 **POSITION OF WINNER IN MARKET** 1113215311

# 5.00 Ascot Stakes

FOUNDED in 1839, this 2m4f handicap has come to be dominated by trainers whose main emphasis is jump racing, with Willie Mullins, Nicky Henderson, Jonjo O'Neill and David Pipe on the roll of honour since 2010.

## Last year's winner

Coltrane came from a pure Flat background and was just outside the ideal range in terms of official rating and recent winning form, but his major plus was he was already a big handicap winner (2022 Melrose) – and he was coming off a neck second in the Chester Cup.

**Form** Four of the last ten winners had scored last time out but another four had been unplaced.

**Weight** Last year's first four all carried 9st 4lb or 9st 5lb after taking into account 5lb

## Key trends

▶ *Won a Flat handicap, 10/10*
▶ *Won within last five Flat starts, 9/10*
▶ *Previously ran over hurdles, 8/10*
▶ *Raced no more than once on the Flat that season, 8/10*
▶ *Officially rated 91-98, 7/10*

## Other factors

▶ *Four winners were set to carry 9st 10lb (last year's winner Coltrane was ridden by a 5lb claimer)*
▶ *Only three winners had scored beyond 2m on the Flat*

rider claims on the winner and third. Four winners and two runners-up have carried top weight of 9st 10lb since 2012.

**Key races** Last year's third, Arcadian Sunrise, also came out of the Chester Cup

(fourth) and 2021 winner Reshoun had prepped by finishing 11th there. Five of the six Irish winners since 2012 had run recently over hurdles at the Punchestown festival. On the Flat, handicaps at Newmarket, York and Leopardstown have also been a stepping stone.

**Trainers** Mullins has had four winners since 2012, as well as the runner-up in 2019, 2021 and 2022 (having not had a representative in 2020). His record since 2012 is 10177011345022002 from 17 runners for a level-stake profit of +14pts.

**Betting** This is not impossibly hard, with half of the last ten winners coming from the top five in the betting. The only two successful favourites in the past 20 years were both trained by Mullins.

## Story of the last ten years

| FORM | WINNER | AGE | & WGT | OR | SP | TRAINER | BEST RPR LAST 12 MONTHS (RUNS SINCE) |
|------|--------|-----|-------|-----|-----|---------|--------------------------------------|
| 22 6-422 | **Coltrane** BF | 5 | 9-5 | 98-3 | 14-1 | Andrew Balding | 2nd Kempton Class 2 hcap (1m4f) (4) |
| 21 600-0 | **Reshoun** | 7 | 9-7 | 97-2 | 66-1 | Ian Williams | won Newbury Class 2 hcap (2m½f) (4) |
| 20 330-5 | **Coeur De Lion** | 7 | 8-10 | 91-3 | 16-1 | Alan King | 3rd Northumberland Vase (2m½f) (3) |
| 19 101-7 | **The Grand Visir** | 5 | 9-10 | 100-3 | 12-1 | Ian Williams | won Doncaster Class 3 hcap (1m6½f) (1) |
| 18 1332- | **Lagostovegas** | 6 | 9-3 | 93-3 | 10-1 | Willie Mullins (IRE) | 2nd Naas Listed (1m4f) (0) |
| 17 1211/ | **Thomas Hobson** | 7 | 9-10 | 100T | 4-1f | Willie Mullins (IRE) | Seasonal debut (0) |
| 16 /21-1 | **Jennies Jewel** | 9 | 9-3 | 93-4 | 6-1 | Jarlath Fahey (IRE) | won Curragh handicap (2m) (0) |
| 15 2101- | **Clondaw Warrior** | 8 | 9-0 | 89-4 | 5-1f | Willie Mullins (IRE) | won Leopardstown handicap (1m7f) (0) |
| 14 120-0 | **Domination** | 7 | 9-7 | 92-3 | 12-1 | Charles Byrnes (IRE) | 2nd Galway handicap (2m) (2) |
| 13 086/1 | **Well Sharp** | 5 | 9-10 | 95-6 | 9-1 | Jonjo O'Neill | won York Class 3 handicap (2m½f) (0) |

**WINS-PL-RUNS** 4yo 0-11-44, 5yo 3-11-60, 6yo+ 7-8-86 **FAVOURITES** £1.00

**FATE OF FAVOURITES** 2510140252 **POSITION OF WINNER IN MARKET** 4712158706

## Story of the last ten years

| FORM | WINNER | AGE & WGT | Adj RPR | SP | TRAINER | BEST RPR LAST 12 MONTHS (RUNS SINCE) |
|---|---|---|---|---|---|---|
| 22  14504 | **Dubai Future** D | 6 9-8 | 121-4 | 20-1 | Saeed bin Suroor | won Meydan Listed (1m4f) (4) |
| 21  438-6 | **Juan Elcano** C, D | 4 9-3 | 119-7 | 14-1 | Kevin Ryan | 3rd Dante Stakes Gp2 (1m2½f) (2) |
| 20  7220- | **Mountain Angel** C, D | 6 9-3 | 122-10 | 8-1 | Roger Varian | 2nd Prix Dollar Gp2 (1m2f) (1) |
| 19  803-4 | **Addeybb** C, BF | 5 9-3 | 125-3 | 5-1 | William Haggas | 3rd Lingfield Listed (1m2f) (1) |
| 18  211-0 | **Monarchs Glen** D | 4 9-8 | 123-3 | 8-1 | John Gosden | won Newmarket Gp3 (1m1f) (1) |
| 17*  8-157 | **Snoano** D | 5 9-0 | 120-4 | 25-1 | Tim Easterby | 5th Huxley Stakes Gp3 (1m2½f) (1) |
| 16*  64-23 | **Sir Issac Newton** | 4 9-0 | 122T | 7-1 | Aidan O'Brien (IRE) | 4th Leopardstown Gp2 (1m) (2) |
| 15*  1-11 | **Mahsoob** D | 4 9-3 | 124-1 | 7-4f | John Gosden | won York Class 2 handicap (1m2½f) (0) |
| 14*  24-13 | **Contributer** D | 4 9-5 | 116-6 | 9-1 | Ed Dunlop | won Kempton Listed (1m2f) (1) |
| 13*  5750/ | **Forgotten Voice** C | 8 9-2 | 124T | 12-1 | Nicky Henderson | Seasonal debut (0) |

*Run as a handicap before 2018

**WINS-RUNS** 4yo 5-13-61, 5yo 2-5-44, 6yo+ 3-3-40 **FAVOURITES** -£7.25

**FATE OF FAVOURITES** 5216052222 **POSITION OF WINNER IN MARKET** 7414042480

Speeding home in last year's Wolferton Stakes

NAUGURATED in 2002 with the extension of Royal Ascot to a five-day meeting, this was changed in 2018 to become a 1m2f Listed conditions race for four-year-olds and up (rather than a Listed handicap).

**Last year's winner**
Godolphin's 20-1 shot Dubai Future (trained by Saeed bin Suroor) became the longest-priced winner since the change in 2018. He had won on a right-handed track before and had the class (as a Listed winner already) but he was older than the norm and drawn in double figures (11).

**Form** All five winners since 2018 had been beaten on their previous start (indeed, none had made the top three) – the most recent-last-time out scorer was Mahsoob in 2015. But all of the last five had been placed at least in a Group contest (two had won at that level).

**Key trends**
▶ *Won on a right-handed track, 9/10*
▶ *Beaten on previous start, 9/10 (three over a different distance to this race)*
▶ *Ran no more than twice that season, 8/10*
▶ *Won at Class 2 level or higher, 8/10*
▶ *Aged four or five, 7/10 (five aged four)*
▶ *Drawn in single figures, 7/10*

**Other factors**
▶ *Seven winners had finished outside the top three last time out*
▶ *John Gosden has won this four times since 2011, including in 2018 (Monarchs Glen) – the first time it was a conditions race rather than a handicap*

**Key races** Four of the five winners since 2018 had run in Listed company at least on their most recent start. Two had run at Meydan over the winter; domestic 1m2f races like the Brigadier Gerard are worth checking.

**Trainers** Dubai Future last year was the fourth winner for a Newmarket yard in five runnings as a Listed race (the town's trainers also took six of the last nine as a handicap). Their stables are well stocked with the later-maturing, well-bred types who do well in this race.

**Betting** The first three winners post-2018 were in the first four in the betting; the last two have been much further down the list.

RUN over 1m6f, this handicap for four-year-olds and upwards was introduced as part of the enhanced programme for Royal Ascot in 2020.

Newmarket stables filled the first three places in the first two runnings, but North Yorkshire trainer David O'Meara struck last year with 16-1 shot Get Shirty.

Seven of the nine runners who have finished in the first three were rated 95-100 (including every winner) and five of them had winning form over at least 1m6f.

Get Shirty scores for David O'Meara last year at 16-1 ahead of 2-1 favourite Cleveland

# Punting tactics – from sires to jockeys

Racing Post deputy betting editor Graeme Rodway examines important evidence from last year's meeting

### IS O'BRIEN ADOPTING THE MULLINS APPROACH?

Most people would agree that Willie Mullins is the best trainer at placing his horses in the right races at the Cheltenham Festival and I've often felt his approach tends to involve finding his best novice and running them in what he perceives is the weakest novice race.

Last year he did that with Sir Gerhard, swerving a clash with Constitution Hill in the Supreme in favour of an easier assignment in the Ballymore, and this season he sent Impaire Et Passe to the same race rather than go for the Supreme, which already looks stronger form.

For years Aidan O'Brien tended to run his best

juvenile in the Coventry, which he has won nine times, but last season his best youngster was definitely Little Big Bear and he contested the Windsor Castle, a race that would traditionally be considered one of the weaker juveniles.

The year before that he had won the Chesham with Point Lonsdale, another race that would often be considered among the weaker juvenile events of the week, and I wonder if O'Brien is now doing a Mullins and aiming his best youngsters at these races rather than the Coventry.

Any Royal Ascot win, no matter what the race, is more valuable for a stallion prospect than no win at all, so I'll be keeping a close eye on the O'Brien representatives in the supposed weaker juvenile events like the Windsor Castle and Chesham. They may be his best chances.

### DUBAWI'S DOMINANCE SHOWS NO SIGN OF RELENTING

In the last five years Galileo and Dubawi are tied for the most Royal Ascot wins by sire on 11, but Dubawi achieved that number from 21 fewer runners and his dominance is set to grow even further now Galileo is no

The draw: don't get hung up on stall numbers

longer around following his death two years ago.

Dubawi's progeny were 5-15 at last year's meeting and his winners included 33-1 shot Naval Crown and 20-1 Dubai Future. Backing the sire's runners would have yielded a £50.40 profit to £1 stakes.

Four of those winners were owned by Godolphin and the leading owner might be capable of even more winners this year as Charlie Appleby's string tends to be very Dubawi heavy.

## THE DRAW CAN CHANGE FROM RACE-TO-RACE AND DAY-TO-DAY

A lot of people get wrapped up in draw analysis on the straight course at Ascot but last year there wasn't a lot in it. Each side of the track was favoured at different times in the week.

Last year's meeting would suggest it goes in waves depending on where the fresh ground is deemed. On Tuesday and Wednesday the majority of the winners raced middle-to-stands side,

Ryan Moore: a better
bet in multiples later
in the week

but by the Britannia at 5pm on Thursday the winners began to come to the middle-to-far side.

If you take away the stall number of each winner and just concentrate on which part of the track they raced, very few who were successful hugged either rail. Most winners raced in the middle of the track to a large degree and I won't be getting hung up on the stall number. The jockey, and how good they are at picking the right horses to follow, looks far more important.

## RYAN MOORE GETS BETTER AS THE WEEK GOES ON

Nobody has ridden more winners at Royal Ascot than Ryan Moore in the last ten years, but he often starts the week comparatively slowly and rides more winners as the week goes on.

The reason for this is probably not down to anything Moore does himself, but more a product of the type of horses he rides and the way the different kinds of races fall through the week.

He has had 55 winners since 2013 and 47 of them came for Aidan O'Brien, Sir Michael Stoute or Willie Mullins. All three of those trainers tend to excel in races that come on Thursday, Friday and Saturday, so Moore thrives as a result of his connection to them.

Last year he rode seven winners across the week, but only one on the first two days. He went on to bang in six across the last three days, so if you're thinking of doing multiple bets including the Moore-ridden runners, you should wait until later in the meeting.

## LOOK FOR EARLY FOALS IN JUVENILE RACES

Most juveniles who run at Royal Ascot this year will have been foaled from January to May 2021 and those born in January outperformed the rest last year. It makes sense as they are up to four months older and therefore likely to be more developed, both physically and mentally.

Backing January-foaled juveniles at last year's Royal Ascot would have netted two winners from eight qualifiers and, while the scorers were only 6-5 hotpot Little Big Bear and 5-2 Meditate, a 25 per cent strike-rate is enough to convince me it's a tactic worth adopting.

# DAY TWO

2.30 **Queen Mary Stakes** (Group 2)
Last year's winner: Dramatised 5-2f
**5f** 2yo fillies
£115,000

3.05 **Kensington Palace Stakes** (Handicap)
Last year's winner: Rising Star 40-1
**1m** 4yo
fillies and mares
£100,000

3.40 **Duke of Cambridge Stakes** (Group 2)
Last year's winner: Saffron Beach 5-2jf
**1m** 4yo+
fillies and mares
£225,000

4.20 **Prince of Wales's Stakes** (Group 1)
Last year's winner: State Of Rest 5-1
**1m2f** 4yo+
£1,000,000

5.00 **Royal Hunt Cup** (Heritage Handicap)
Last year's winner: Dark Shift 13-2
**1m** 3yo+
£175,000

5.35 **Queen's Vase** (Group 2)
Last year's winner: Eldar Eldarov 5-2f
**1m6f** 3yo
£265,000

6.10 **Windsor Castle Stakes** (Listed)
Last year's winner: Little Big Bear 6-5f
**5f** 2yo
£100,000

Race value is total prize-money

34

The Group 1 Prince of Wales's Stakes takes top billing on a day that also features a historic big-field handicap, emerging stayers and two-year-old flyers.

Run over a mile and a quarter for four-year-olds and upwards, the Prince of Wales's was revived in its current format in 1968 and this will be the first running since the title passed to Prince William on the accession to the throne of King Charles.

Ever since Derby hero Royal Palace took the prize in that return year, this race has had a Classic quality for older horses. Brigadier Gerard (1972) and Dubai Millennium (2000) are just two of the big names on the star-studded roll of honour,

along with later developers such as 1980s dual winner Mtoto.

Last year the Joseph O'Brien-trained State Of Rest became Ireland's eighth winner since 1968 and there have been five successes for France (most recently Byword in 2010) in a race that showcases the cream of European talent.

The card opens with the Queen Mary Stakes, the meeting's premier race for two-year-old fillies and one of three Group 2s on the card. Last year Dramatised proved a typically high-class winner, later going close in the Breeders' Cup Juvenile Turf Sprint.

This year the Kensington Palace Stakes, a handicap for four-year-old fillies and mares run around the bend on the Old Mile. moves up

to second on the card.

The focus stays on older fillies and mares in the Group 2 Duke of Cambridge Stakes, this time over the straight mile.

After the main feature comes the Royal Hunt Cup, the first of the week's heritage handicaps. A field of up to 30 runners will charge down the straight mile in this fierce battle for three-year-olds and upwards.

The emphasis switches from speedsters to stayers in the Group 2 Queen's Vase, the day's longest race over a mile and three-quarters. Last year's winner Eldar Eldarov went on to land the St Leger.

Then the fast and early two-year-olds have another turn over five furlongs in the Listed Windsor Castle Stakes, which unlike the Queen Mary is open to both sexes.

FOUNDED in honour of the consort of King George V and first run in 1921, this five-furlong dash is the premier race at the meeting restricted to two-year-old fillies – the only other of that ilk is the Albany Stakes, which is run over six furlongs on Friday and is a step lower than this Group 2.

## Last year's winner

Dramatised fitted all the key trends and scored by a length and three-quarters in a strong form race. She ended her season with a close second in the Grade 1 Breeders' Cup Juvenile Turf Sprint and The Platinum Queen (13th here) went on to win the Group 1 Prix de l'Abbaye.

**Form** High-class winning form is virtually essential and 11 of the 14 winners since

## Key trends

▶ By a sire with a stamina index between 5.9f and 8.4f, ten winners in last ten runnings
▶ Top-three finish last time out, 10/10 (eight won)
▶ Adjusted Racing Post Rating of at least 103, 9/10
▶ Rated within 9lb of RPR top-rated, 8/10
▶ Distance winner, 6/10

## Other factors

▶ Two of the four not to have won over the trip were trained by Wesley Ward – one had won over 4½f, while the other was still a maiden

2009 had scored last time out – two of the three exceptions were trained by US raider Wesley Ward (Jealous Again and Acapulco), along with 2021

winner Quick Suzy, who had been runner-up in a Group 3.

**Key races** The Marygate Stakes at York is the main northern stepping stone, with Ceiling Kitty (2012) and Signora Cabello (2018) the most recent to double up. Ward likes to prep his juveniles at Keeneland, often over four and a half furlongs.

**Trainers** Ward has had four of the 14 winners since he started to target Royal Ascot in 2009 as well as three beaten favourites (two of his last three winners also headed the market).

**Betting** Nine of the last 14 winners were in the top three in the betting and it is worth noting that three of the longer-priced winners came from northern stables (even though two of them had high-class winning form in the Marygate at York).

| | FORM | WINNER | AGE & WGT | Adj RPR | SP | TRAINER | BEST RPR LAST 12 MONTHS (RUNS SINCE) |
|---|---|---|---|---|---|---|---|
| 22 | 1 | **Dramatised** D | 2 9-2 | 113$^T$ | 5-2f | Karl Burke | won Newmarket Class 3 maiden (5f) (0) |
| 21 | 212 | **Quick Suzy** | 2 9-0 | 108$^{-2}$ | 8-1 | Gavin Cromwell (IRE) | 2nd Naas Gp3 (6f) (0) |
| 20 | 1 | **Campanelle** D | 2 9-0 | 104$^{-3}$ | 9-2 | Wesley Ward (USA) | won Gulfstream maiden (5f) (0) |
| 19 | 21 | **Raffle Prize** | 2 9-0 | 103$^{-12}$ | 18-1 | Mark Johnston | won Chester Class 2 maiden (6f) (0) |
| 18 | 411 | **Signora Cabella** D | 2 9-0 | 105$^{-7}$ | 25-1 | John Quinn | won York Listed (5f) (0) |
| 17 | 1 | **Heartache** D | 2 9-0 | 107$^{-3}$ | 5-1 | Clive Cox | won Bath Class 4 novice (5f) (0) |
| 16 | 1 | **Lady Aurelia** | 2 9-0 | 112$^T$ | 2-1f | Wesley Ward (USA) | won Keeneland maiden (4½f) (0) |
| 15 | 3 | **Acapulco** BF | 2 9-0 | 91$^{-15}$ | 5-2f | Wesley Ward (USA) | 3rd Churchill Downs maiden (4½f) (0) |
| 14 | 61 | **Anthem Alexander** D | 2 9-0 | 106$^{-9}$ | 9-4f | Eddie Lynam (IRE) | won Tipperary maiden (5f) (0) |
| 13 | 511 | **Rizeena** CD | 2 8-12 | 112$^T$ | 6-1 | Clive Brittain | won Sandown Listed (5f) (0) |

**FAVOURITES** £3.25

**TRAINERS IN THIS RACE** (w-pl-r) Wesley Ward 3-4-13, Karl Burke 1-0-4, Clive Cox 1-1-9, Richard Hannon 0-2-10, Aidan O'Brien 0-1-8, Jessica Harrington 0-0-2, William Haggas 0-2-4, Andrew Balding 0-0-2, Richard Fahey 0-0-10

**FATE OF FAVOURITES** 0111203021 **POSITION OF WINNER IN MARKET** 3111290221

Rising Star takes last year's
Kensington Palace at 40-1

NOW in its third year, this mile handicap is run over the round course for older fillies and mares rated 0-105 and has proved a tricky test for punters. Dave Loughnane had the first two (Lola Showgirl at 12-1 and Ffion at 10-1) in the inaugural running and both had got in at the bottom end of the weights off ratings of 81, while last year the first three were Marco Botti's Rising Star (40-1), Random Harvest (40-1) and Isola Rossa (22-1). The draw may have been a factor last year, with the first three coming from stalls 17, 22 and 18, but in the inaugural running the first three were drawn ten, two and four.

THIS Group 2 contest for older fillies and mares is run over the straight mile and was introduced in 2004 with the aim of encouraging connections to keep female runners in training beyond their three-year-old campaigns.

## Last year's winner

Saffron Beach, having competed almost exclusively in Group 1s for the previous year, dropped back a notch to take victory by three and a half lengths as the 5-2 joint-favourite. She fulfilled the main criteria apart from a top-three finish last time out, albeit she had been fourth in the Group 1 Dubai Turf.

**Form** High-class form is important, with the majority of winners having scored already at Group level. Saffron Beach had ended the previous season with victory

### Key trends
- *Distance winner, 9/10*
- *Rated within 6lb of RPR top-rated, 8/10*
- *Top-three finish that season, 7/10 (one exception making reappearance)*
- *Adjusted RPR of at least 121, 8/10*
- *Had won a Group race, 7/10*

### Other factors
- *Winners of the Dahlia at Newmarket finished 39412*
- *Three winners had run at the previous year's meeting – one in the Sandringham (1), one in the Coronation (1) and one in this race (2)*

in the Group 1 Sun Chariot Stakes, although in contrast none of the three winners immediately before her had been successful at Group

level. Qemah in 2017 was another previous Group 1 winner. Saffron Beach was the first to defy a Group 1 penalty, being the 17th to try.

**Key races** The Snowdrop Fillies' Stakes at Kempton has been used as a stepping stone from all-weather to turf in recent years. Turf races to note are the Dahlia Stakes at Newmarket and the previous year's Atalanta Stakes at Sandown.

**Trainers** John Gosden (latterly in partnership with son Thady) and Sir Michael Stoute have each had four winners.

**Betting** Saffron Beach became the sixth successful favourite or joint-favourite in the 19 runnings. Seven of the last ten winners came from the top three in the betting.

### Story of the last ten years

| | FORM | WINNER | AGE & WGT | Adj RPR | SP | TRAINER | BEST RPR LAST 12 MONTHS (RUNS SINCE) |
|---|---|---|---|---|---|---|---|
| 22 | 011-4 | **Saffron Beach** D | 4 9-7 | $125^3$ | 5-2j | Jane Chapple-Hyam | won Sun Chariot Gp1 (1m) (1) |
| 21 | 71-54 | **Indie Angel** D | 4 9-0 | $119^{11}$ | 22-1 | John & Thady Gosden | won Lingfield Listed (1m) (2) |
| 20 | 111-1 | **Nazeef** D | 4 9-0 | $121^4$ | 10-3 | John Gosden | won Newmarket Class 3 hcap (1m) (1) |
| 19 | 1222- | **Move Swiftly** D, BF | 4 9-0 | $122^6$ | 9-1 | William Haggas | 2nd Newmarket Class 2 hcap (1m) (1) |
| 18 | 197-3 | **Aljazzi** D | 5 9-0 | $128^T$ | 9-2 | Marco Botti | won Atalanta Stakes Gp3 (1m) (3) |
| 17 | 113-2 | **Qemah** C, D | 4 9-0 | $131^T$ | 5-2f | Jean-Claude Rouget (FR) | won Prix Rothschild Gp1 (1m) (2) |
| 16 | 7-111 | **Usherette** D | 4 9-3 | $128^{-1}$ | 9-4f | Andre Fabre (FR) | won Dahlia Stakes Gp2 (1m1f) (0) |
| 15 | 00-33 | **Amazing Maria** | 4 9-0 | $119^9$ | 25-1 | David O'Meara | 3rd Lanwades Stud Stakes Gp2 (1m) (0) |
| 14 | 712-2 | **Integral** D, BF | 4 9-0 | $130^T$ | 9-4f | Sir Michael Stoute | 2nd Sun Chariot Stakes Gp1 (1m) (1) |
| 13 | 11d-1 | **Duntle** CD | 4 8-12 | $131^{-1}$ | 10-3 | David Wachman (IRE) | 2nd Matron Stakes Gp1 (1m) (1) |

**WINS-PL-RUNS** 4yo 9-11-87, 5yo 1-7-21, 6yo+ 0-0-6 **FAVOURITES** £0.69

**TRAINERS IN THIS RACE** (w-pl-r) Sir Michael Stoute 1-4-10, Andre Fabre 1-1-3, David O'Meara 1-2-5, Marco Botti 1-1-2, John & Thady Gosden 1-0-1, William Haggas 1-0-4, Aidan O'Brien 0-1-4, Charlie Appleby 0-0-2, Charlie Varian 0-0-8

**FATE OF FAVOURITES** 6151103331 **POSITION OF WINNER IN MARKET** 2151126381

FIRST run in 1862 and reduced in distance to a mile and a quarter on its revival in 1968, this Group 1 showpiece is often the top-ranked contest of Royal Ascot, based on the ratings of the first four finishers.

**Last year's winner** State Of Rest was the lowest rated of the five runners yet only 5lb off top on adjusted Racing Post Ratings and was strong on the other key trends. He beat 10-11 favourite Bay Bridge by a length.

**Form** The typical winner has already proved top class, both in terms of races won and ratings achieved, and only six winners in the 23 runnings since the race was promoted to elite status in 2000 were scoring at Group 1 level for the first time. It is interesting that all six have

struck in the last 13 editions (Byword, Free Eagle, My Dream Boat, Poet's Word, Crystal Ocean and Lord North), although it is equally worth noting that most of those had strong Group 1 placings already.

**Key races** Since 2000 Poet's Word, Crystal Ocean and Lord North are the only ones of the 20 winners who had already raced that season not to have posted their most recent outing at Group 1 level, although a trial to note at a lower level is the Group 3 Gordon Richards Stakes at Sandown (won by Al Kazeem in 2013, My Dream Boat in 2016 and Crystal Ocean in 2019). Another significant Group 3 is the Brigadier Gerard Stakes, also at Sandown, which was won by Poet's Word in 2018 after his earlier good run in Group 1 company when second in

the Dubai Sheema Classic at Meydan and by Lord North in 2020 (when it was run at Haydock).

Horses coming off a break after a good performance on Dubai World Cup night also

## Story of the last ten years

| | FORM | WINNER | AGE & WGT | Adj RPR | SP | TRAINER | BEST RPR LAST 12 MONTHS (RUNS SINCE) |
|---|---|---|---|---|---|---|---|
| 22 | 11-13 | **State Of Rest** D, BF | 4 9-2 | 133-5 | 5-1 | Joseph O'Brien (IRE) | won Cox Plate Gp1 (1m2f) (2) |
| 21 | /111- | **Love** | 4 8-11 | 141T | 11-10f | Aidan O'Brien (IRE) | won Yorkshire Oaks Gp1 (1m4f) (0) |
| 20 | 121-1 | **Lord North** D | 4 9-0 | 135-4 | 5-1 | John Gosden | won Brigadier Gerard Gp3 (1m2f) (0) |
| 19 | 22-11 | **Crystal Ocean** C, D | 5 9-0 | 141T | 3-1 | Sir Michael Stoute | 2nd King George Gp1 (1m4f) (4) |
| 18 | 26-21 | **Poet's Word** D | 5 9-0 | 134-11 | 11-2 | Sir Michael Stoute | 2nd Irish Champion Gp1 (1m2f) (4) |
| 17 | 12-71 | **Highland Reel** C, D | 5 9-0 | 138-1 | 9-4 | Aidan O'Brien (IRE) | 2nd Prix de l'Arc de Triomphe Gp1 (1m4f) (4) |
| 16 | 11-15 | **My Dream Boat** D | 4 9-0 | 134-11 | 16-1 | Clive Cox | won Gordon Richards Gp3 (1m2f) (1) |
| 15 | 2/13- | **Free Eagle** D | 4 9-0 | 136-4 | 5-2f | Dermot Weld (IRE) | 3rd Champion Stakes Gp1 (1m2f) (0) |
| 14 | 122-0 | **The Fugue** D | 5 8-11 | 140-8 | 11-2 | John Gosden | won Irish Champion Gp1 (1m2f) (3) |
| 13 | /1-11 | **Al Kazeem** D | 5 9-0 | 137T | 11-4 | Roger Charlton | won Tattersalls Gold Cup Gp1 (1m2½f) (0) |

**WINS-PL-RUNS** 4yo 5-11-38, 5yo 5-3-23, 6yo+ 0-1-14 **FAVOURITES** -£4.40

**TRAINERS IN THIS RACE** (w-pl-r) Aidan O'Brien 2-3-12, Sir Michael Stoute 2-2-8, Andre Fabre 0-1-1, Andrew Balding 0-0-2, Charlie Appleby 0-0-4, Roger Varian 0-0-2, Saeed bin Suroor 0-0-1, William Haggas 0-2-5, John & Thady Gosden 0-0-1

**FATE OF FAVOURITES** 4316822412 **POSITION OF WINNER IN MARKET** 2216222313

# 4.20 Prince of Wales's Stakes

## Key trends
- ▶ *Adjusted RPR of at least 133, 10/10*
- ▶ *Aged four or five, 10/10*
- ▶ *Distance winner, 9/10*
- ▶ *Rated within 8lb of RPR top-rated, 8/10*
- ▶ *Between seven and 17 career runs, 7/10*

## Other factors
- ▶ *Thirteen fillies have gone to post, finishing 3135242566213*
- ▶ *Since Rakti in 2004, two winners landed the prize on their reappearance (Free Eagle in 2015 and Love in 2021)*
- ▶ *Five winners had previously landed a Group 1*

have a decent record, with The Fugue in 2014 the most recent of four such winners this century.

The Tattersalls Gold Cup has been the chosen warm-up for six winners during that period (among that number only Azamour in 2005 and State Of Rest last year were beaten at the Curragh), while France's two early-season Group 1s, the Prix d'Ispahan and the Prix Ganay, have been a launch pad for four winners between them.

State Of Rest (left) scores last year for Joseph O'Brien (below)

**Trainers** The most successful current trainers are Aidan O'Brien, Sir Michael Stoute and Saeed bin Suroor on four wins. Sir Henry Cecil holds the record with five.

**Betting** In a sign that the cream rises to the top, only two of the 23 winners since 2000 were outside the top three in the betting.

## Roll of honour
**Longest-priced winner**
Bob Back 33-1 (1985)

**Shortest-priced winner**
Royal Palace 1-4 (1968)

**Most successful trainer**
5 wins: **Sir Henry Cecil**
Lucky Wednesday (1977), Gunner B (1978), Perpendicular (1992), Placerville (1993), Bosra Sham (1997)

**Most successful jockey**
5 wins: **Pat Eddery**
Record Run (1975), English Spring (1986), Two Timing (1989), Batshoof (1990), Placerville (1993)

**Most successful owner**
5 wins: **Godolphin**
Faithful Son (1998), Dubai Millennium (2000), Fantastic Light (2001), Grandera (2002), Rewilding (2011)

*All figures since 1968

# 5.00 Royal Hunt Cup

FIRST run in 1843, this is the first of the week's heritage handicaps to feature a cavalry charge down the straight course, with 30 runners fanning out in the mile contest for three-year-olds and up.

**Last year's winner** Dark Shift, running under a 5lb penalty but 2lb well in on official ratings, was second favourite at 13-2 and hit nearly every key trend (falling a tad below on size of field won in).

**Form** Most recent winners arrived off the back of a top-four finish, though rarely after a victory, and had some big-field experience.

**Draw** With the majority of recent winners having come from the highest ten stalls, the near side is often the place to be.

**Key races** The Lincoln, Spring Cup and Victoria

**Key trends**
▶ Aged four or five, 9/10 (seven aged four)
▶ Officially rated between 96 and 103, 8/10
▶ Carried between 8st 11lb and 9st 3lb, 8/10
▶ Won or been placed in a field of at least 13 runners, 8/10
▶ Top-three finish at least once that season, 8/10 (both exceptions making reappearance)
▶ Ran between one and four times that campaign, 8/10
▶ Rated within 3lb of RPR

top-rated, 7/10
▶ Distance winner, 6/10

**Other factors**
▶ There have been only three winning favourites in the last 34 years – True Panache in 1989, Yeast in 1996 and Forgotten Voice in 2009
▶ Only three of the last ten winners were drawn in single figures, while last year's winner Dark Shift was the only one drawn between stalls 12 and 20
▶ Four winners wore some form of headgear

Cup provide a road map, but perhaps most notably six of the last ten winners had run in a Cambridgeshire at Newmarket or the Curragh the previous year.

**Trainers** With Dark Shift last year adding to Afaak's success in 2019, Charlie Hills became only the fourth

trainer with more than a single win this century.

**Betting** The market has been no better than a fair guide, with seven of the 13 winners outside the top seven in the betting since the gambled-on Forgotten Voice was the last winning favourite in 2009.

## Story of the last ten years

| | FORM | WINNER | | AGE & WGT | OR | SP | TRAINER | BEST RPR LAST 12 MONTHS (RUNS SINCE) |
|---|---|---|---|---|---|---|---|---|
| 22 | 11-01 | **Dark Shift** | (5ex) CD | 4 9-1 | 96·1 | 13-2 | Charles Hills | won Nottingham Class 2 hcap (1m½f) (0) |
| 21 | 2-334 | **Real World** | | 4 8-6 | 94·6 | 18-1 | Saeed Bin Suroor | 3rd Meydan Listed hcap (1m2f) (1) |
| 20 | 630-2 | **Dark Vision** | BF | 4 9-1 | 100ᵀ | 15-2 | Mark Johnston | 2nd Newcastle Class 2 hcap (1m) (0) |
| 19 | 4630- | **Afaak** | D | 5 9-3 | 103·3 | 20-1 | Charlie Hills | 2nd Royal Hunt Cup (1m) (4) |
| 18 | 11-14 | **Settle For Bay** | D | 4 9-1 | 99·8 | 16-1 | David Marnane (IRE) | 4th Leopardstown hcap (7f) (0) |
| 17 | -4803 | **Zhui Feng** | | 4 9-0 | 100·3 | 25-1 | Amanda Perrett | 4th Winter Derby Gp3 (1m2f) (3) |
| 16 | 125-1 | **Portage** | (5ex) CD | 4 9-5 | 105·7 | 10-1 | Mick Halford (IRE) | 5th Newmarket Class 2 hcap (1m1f) (1) |
| 15 | 43-02 | **Gm Hopkins** | D, BF | 4 9-3 | 103·2 | 8-1 | John Gosden | 2nd Newbury Class 2 hcap (1m) (0) |
| 14 | 5950- | **Field Of Dream** | C | 7 9-1 | 101·1 | 20-1 | Jamie Osborne | won Newmarket Class 2 hcap (7f) (4) |
| 13 | -0020 | **Belgian Bill** | D | 5 8-11 | 97·2 | 33-1 | George Baker | won Kempton Class 2 hcap (7f) (6) |

**WINS-PL-RUNS** 4yo 7-17-123, 5yo 2-5-69, 6yo+ 1-8-91 **FAVOURITES** -£10.00

**FATE OF FAVOURITES** 0000005020 **POSITION OF WINNER IN MARKET** 0823090392

DATING back to 1838 and run under its current name since 1960, this Group 2 over 1m6f is restricted to three-year-olds and designed to bring along future St Leger and Cup horses over staying trips. This is the seventh year since a reduction in distance from two miles.

**Last year's winner** Eldar Eldarov missed out on just one key trend (his sire, Dubawi, fell a bit short of the optimum stamina index) and got up on the line to edge out 20-1 shot Zechariah. He went on to land the St Leger, becoming the latest high-class winner since the reduction in distance following top stayer Stradivarius (2017), Kew Gardens (2018; St Leger) and Santiago (2020; Irish Derby).

**Key trends**
▶ *Top-three finish last time out, 9/10*
▶ *By a sire with a stamina index in excess of 1m2f, 8/10*
▶ *Adjusted RPR of at least 108, 8/10*
▶ *Won within last two starts, 7/10*
▶ *Rated within 8lb of RPR top-rated, 7/10*

**Other factors**
▶ *The only trainers to have won this race since 2000 are Sir Michael Stoute (three times), Saeed bin Suroor (twice), Mark Johnston (seven), Aidan O'Brien (seven), John Gosden, Andrew Balding, Charlie Appleby and Roger Varian (all once)*
▶ *Five winners ran in a Listed or Group race last time out*

**Form** Winning form is not essential, given that some will come here after being tried down the Classics route, although four of the last ten winners had scored last time out. Half of the winners in the past decade had run in Group company (four at the top level).

**Key races** Aidan O'Brien is likely to send one or more of his lesser lights from the Classics trail, while British winners tend to come from a more low-key route through maidens and even handicaps.

**Trainers** The race has been monopolised by stables with the best resources for staying and middle-distance horses.

**Betting** The market is often a good guide to the best prospects from the big stables, with 12 of the last 15 winners coming from the top two in the betting.

## Story of the last ten years

| | FORM | WINNER | AGE & WGT | Adj RPR | SP | TRAINER | BEST RPR LAST 12 MONTHS (RUNS SINCE) |
|---|---|---|---|---|---|---|---|
| 22 | 1-1 | **Eldar Eldarov** | 3 9-2 | 111-8 | 5-2f | Roger Varian | won Newcastle Class 5 novice (1m2f) (0) |
| 21 | 21 | **Kemari** | 3 9-0 | 108-12 | 15-2 | Charlie Appleby | won Yarmouth Class 4 mdn (1m3½f) (0) |
| 20 | 221- | **Santiago** | 3 9-0 | 102-18 | 10-3 | Aidan O'Brien (IRE) | 2nd Galway maiden auction (7f) (1) |
| 19 | 28-23 | **Dashing Willoughby** | 3 9-0 | 118-8 | 6-1 | Andrew Balding | 2nd Newbury Class 3 cond (1m2f) (1) |
| 18 | 1-329 | **Kew Gardens** | 3 9-0 | 121-7 | 10-3 | Aidan O'Brien (IRE) | won Newmarket Listed (1m2f) (3) |
| 17 | 41-12 | **Stradivarius** BF | 3 9-0 | 114-3 | 11-2 | John Gosden | 2nd Chester Class 3 hcap (1m4½f) (0) |
| 16 | 3-213 | **Sword Fighter** | 3 9-3 | 99-16 | 33-1 | Aidan O'Brien (IRE) | 3rd Naas cond (1m4f) (0) |
| 15 | 212- | **Aloft** | 3 9-3 | 123T | 5-2f | Aidan O'Brien (IRE) | 2nd Racing Post Trophy Gp1 (1m) (0) |
| 14 | 13-52 | **Hartnell** | 3 9-3 | 115T | 7-2 | Mark Johnston | 2nd Lingfield Derby Trial Listed (1m3½f) (0) |
| 13 | 41-11 | **Leading Light** | 3 9-4 | 121-T | 5-4f | Aidan O'Brien (IRE) | won Gallinule Stakes Gp3 (1m2f) (0) |

**FAVOURITES** -£0.75

**TRAINERS IN THIS RACE** (w-pl-r) Aidan O'Brien 5-5-21, Roger Varian 1-0-2, Andrew Balding 1-2-9, Charlie Appleby 1-3-3, Sir Michael Stoute 0-0-2, William Haggas 0-0-4, John & Thady Gosden 0-1-5

**FATE OF FAVOURITES** 1314400421 **POSITION OF WINNER IN MARKET** 1210222321

ESTABLISHED in 1839, this Listed five-furlong dash for two-year-olds is open to colts, geldings and fillies.

**Last year's winner** Little Big Bear became only the fifth successful favourite this century when scoring at 6-5 by a neck from 14-1 shot Rocket Rodney. He had the right credentials, apart from the poor record of the RPR top-rated (he was 12lb clear), and was soon a Group 1 winner in the Phoenix Stakes.

**Form** Most winners had a decent level of form, with five of the last nine having been tried in Listed company, although two of the last four went against the established trend in not having lost their maiden tag before coming here.

**Key races** The high-level route involves a Listed

## Key trends
▶ *By a sire with a stamina index of 6.5f-8.1f, 9/10*
▶ *Lost maiden tag, 8/10*
▶ *Ran two or three times, 8/10*
▶ *Adjusted RPR of at least 97, 7/10*

## Other factors
▶ *Fillies won five in a row from 1996 to 2000 but only one has placed in the last ten years*
▶ *Last year's winner Little Big Bear was RPR top-rated, but six of the other nine were between 7lb and 14lb off top*

contest (five of the last ten winners had run in the National at Sandown, the Marble Hill at the Curragh or in a US Listed); the other path is through maidens and novices.

**Trainers** It is notable that ten current trainers achieved their first Royal Ascot success in this contest, most recently Archie Watson with 12-1 shot Soldier's Call in 2018. Perhaps the less high-profile stables save their best hopes for this contest, knowing that the big guns will aim their main fire at the more important juvenile races.

**Betting** This has proved the juvenile race most open to a surprise result in recent years, with nine of the last 17 winners having been 12-1 or bigger. Even the major stables can produce a long-odds winner – Charlie Appleby at 16-1 in 2017 and John Gosden at 20-1 the year before that – and half of the last ten winners came from outside the top six in the betting.

## Story of the last ten years

| | FORM | WINNER | AGE | & WGT | Adj RPR | SP | TRAINER | BEST RPR LAST 12 MONTHS (RUNS SINCE) |
|---|---|---|---|---|---|---|---|---|
| 22 | 21 | **Little Big Bear** D | 2 | 9-5 | 115$^T$ | 6-5f | Aidan O'Brien (IRE) | won Naas maiden (5f) (0) |
| 21 | 116 | **Chipotle** CD | 2 | 9-3 | 99$^{.7}$ | 22-1 | Eve Johnson Houghton | won Ascot Class 2 cond (5f) (1) |
| 20 | 3 | **Tactical** | 2 | 9-3 | 95$^{.3}$ | 7-2f | Andrew Balding | 3rd Newmarket Class 5 novice (5f) (0) |
| 19 | 52 | **Southern Hills** | 2 | 9-3 | 105$^{.4}$ | 7-1 | Aidan O'Brien (IRE) | 2nd Navan maiden (5f) (0) |
| 18 | 21 | **Soldier's Call** D | 2 | 9-3 | 97$^{.14}$ | 12-1 | Archie Watson | won Haydock Class 4 novice (5f) (0) |
| 17 | 14 | **Sound And Silence** D | 2 | 9-3 | 101$^{.11}$ | 16-1 | Charlie Appleby | 4th Sandown Listed (5f) (0) |
| 16 | 1 | **Ardad** D | 2 | 9-3 | 94$^{.14}$ | 20-1 | John Gosden | won Yarmouth Class 4 novice (5f) (0) |
| 15 | 212 | **Washington DC** D, BF | 2 | 9-3 | 106$^{.2}$ | 5-1 | Aidan O'Brien (IRE) | 2nd Curragh Listed (5f) (0) |
| 14 | 13 | **Hootenanny** BF | 2 | 9-3 | 95$^{.13}$ | 7-2f | Wesley Ward (USA) | 3rd Pimlico Listed (5f) (0) |
| 13 | 14 | **Extortionist** D | 2 | 9-3 | 98$^{.10}$ | 16-1 | Olly Stevens | won Nottingham Class 5 maiden (5f) (1) |

**FAVOURITES** £1.20

**TRAINERS IN THIS RACE** (w-pl-r) Aidan O'Brien 3-1-13, Wesley Ward 1-0-14, Andrew Balding 1-0-5, Charlie Appleby 1-1-3, Archie Watson 1-1-13, Eve Johnson Houghton 1-0-4, Kevin Ryan 0-2-3, David O'Meara 0-1-7, Richard Fahey 0-2-9, William Haggas 0-2-4, Roger Varian 0-0-5, Clive Cox, 0-0-3, Richard Hannon 0-0-12

**FATE OF FAVOURITES** 3130004171 **POSITION OF WINNER IN MARKET** 9120773101

# EXPERT VIEW

## Racing Post tipsters pick their early fancies

### COLTRANE
**Gold Cup**

Coltrane won the Ascot Stakes off a mark of 98 a year ago, but such has been his improvement since (officially 19lb) that he has to be a huge player in the Gold Cup this time.

He loves the track (form figures of 121) and his one defeat there was last October when the fading force that is Trueshan beat him by a tiny margin.

His recent Sagaro win was full of authority and he doesn't seem to have any chinks in his armour.
**Nick Watts**

### DEVIOUS
**Norfolk Stakes**

The post-race comments of Donnacha O'Brien after Devious's emphatic winning debut at Naas in early May were almost as striking as the display in a maiden that already looks strong form.

"We have nothing that can take him off the bridle at home," the trainer proclaimed, before adding: "He's a proper horse and shouldn't be so fast given how big he is."

The Starspangledbanner colt was in his comfort zone every step of the way over 5f at Naas and the natural speed he showed suggests the Norfolk is the race for him rather than the Coventry. **David Jennings**

### ELDAR ELDAROV
**Gold Cup**

Roger Varian's four-year-old knows how to win at Royal Ascot, having secured a thrilling last-gasp success in the 1m6f Queen's Vase last year. He improved significantly on that form when outstaying the later demoted Haskoy by two lengths in the St Leger and is expected to make further progress stepped up to 2m4f in the Gold Cup.

He has landed four of his seven starts and appeals strongly as a champion stayer in waiting.
**Richard Birch**

### HIGHFIELD PRINCESS
**King's Stand Stakes**

For most of the Duke of York Stakes, John Quinn's Highfield Princess (below) looked to be running all over her rivals and, while she succumbed to Azure Blue at the line, I'm convinced she was the one to take from the race.

She had to give 5lb to the winner, the market vibes weren't positive for her reappearance, yet she produced a performance that screamed class until lack of a run told close home.

With that race under her belt, I want to be with her for the King's Stand whatever else turns up.
**Nick Watts**

### JUMBLY
**Duke of Cambridge Stakes**

The Duke of Cambridge is one of those Royal Ascot races that threatens to be top class but often isn't, so it's worth looking for a filly who has been aimed at the race all season. Jumbly

stands out on that score like a sore thumb.

She was a Group 3 winner when trained by the Charltons but there is loads of untapped potential and the Coolmore team paid a lot of money for her last November.

Now trained by Joseph O'Brien, she has been set this target and I don't think we have seen anything like the best of her yet. **Tom Segal**

## KINGDOM COME
**Royal Hunt Cup**

This Clive Cox-trained four-year-old has the look of a monster improver who will flourish in a huge-field, straight-mile handicap at Royal Ascot.

Unbeaten in three races over 7f at Kempton this year, he was set to go for Ascot's Victoria Cup in May until connections decided not to risk him on soft ground.

Horses who thrive at Kempton often enjoy the demands of a fast-ground Ascot and Kingdom Come is one to keep firmly on side for the Royal Hunt Cup. He boasts bags of potential when stepped up to a mile. **Richard Birch**

## LEZOO
**Commonwealth Cup**

Tahiyra might have been the top juvenile filly for many last year, but Lezoo held strong claims as she was close to unbeatable.

Her one loss came against now 1,000 Guineas winner Mawj in a tactical race at Newmarket's July meeting and she reversed that form when landing the Cheveley Park on the Rowley Mile. Subsequent Breeders' Cup winner Meditate was second with Mawj third.

Lezoo didn't stay a mile on soft ground in the 1,000 Guineas at Newmarket on her reappearance, but has top-class potential when returned to sprinting for her next run. **Graeme Rodway**

## MAXIMUM IMPACT
**Coventry Stakes**

Alice Haynes's chance of winning big juvenile races at Royal Ascot has gone up now she is backed by leading owners Amo Racing and they have a superb chance of winning the Coventry with this grey colt.

Maximum Impact won by 12 lengths on his debut at Leicester in April and looked even better when staying on strongly to beat previous winner Action Point by two and a quarter lengths at Ascot last time.

He displayed a long stride that day and turned it over quickly, which means he covered a lot of ground fast. That is often the sign of a top-class performer and the step up to 6f will suit. **Graeme Rodway**

## SOPRANO
**Queen Mary/Albany Stakes**

No doubt the Americans will come in

numbers and there will be a draw advantage of some description but at this stage no juvenile filly has impressed me more than George Boughey's Soprano.

Extremely well backed in the Newmarket maiden that produced last year's Queen Mary winner, Soprano was a bit keen early on but showed an impressive turn of foot and hit the line strongly to win by almost two lengths.

She has the option of going 5f or 6f, but wherever she runs it will take a top-class filly to beat her. **Tom Segal**

## TENEBRISM
**Queen Elizabeth II Jubilee Stakes**

Aidan O'Brien says this is the first season where Tenebrism is being treated as an out-and-out sprinter and she catches my eye for Saturday's 6f Group 1.

She doesn't have the instant acceleration for the minimum trip, as we saw at Naas in April when failing to catch Moss Tucker, but a strongly run 6f at a track like Ascot ought to bring out the best in her.

She ran a cracker in last year's Champions Sprint over course and distance, finishing second of 11 in her group with the first three coming from the other group, and we could see a different filly as a four-year-old. **David Jennings**

# DAY THREE

Gold Cup day is very much the centrepiece of the five-day meeting and the main event is the staying highlight of the racing year. Also known as Ladies' Day, the occasion is just as important in the social season. It is an afternoon rich in anticipation and colour.

Established in 1807, the Gold Cup is the meeting's oldest race and one of the longest at two and a half miles. In recent years the Group 1 contest has enjoyed a resurgence in popularity, thanks in large part to royal winner Estimate and hat-trick hero Stradivarius, and consolidated its place at the heart of Royal Ascot's traditions.

Every other race on the card is at least a mile shorter but they combine to make another varied and absorbing mix.

The mile-and-a-half contests are the King George V Stakes, a handicap for three-year-olds that is usually won by a lightly raced improver from a powerful stable, and the Group 2 Ribblesdale Stakes. This is the meeting's middle-distance feature for three-year-old fillies and often attracts graduates from the Oaks at Epsom or at least one of the trials.

Speed is injected by the Group 2 Norfolk Stakes for two-year-olds over the minimum trip of five furlongs. This contest lasts barely 60 seconds, compared with the near four and a half minutes it takes to complete the Gold Cup.

The showpiece race is followed by the Britannia Stakes, a heritage handicap that is basically a Royal Hunt Cup for three-year-old colts and geldings. A high-grade performer, often one capable of winning in Group company, is likely to emerge at the front of a maximum field of 30 down the straight mile.

Race six is the Hampton Court Stakes, a Group 3 for three-year-olds over a mile and a quarter that also often showcases an up-and-coming star.

The final race is the Buckingham Palace Stakes, a seven-furlong handicap that lost its place at the meeting for five years but was reinstated in 2020 as part of the expansion to seven races per day.

# Thursday June 22

## RUNNING ORDER

| | | |
|---|---|---|
| 2.30 **Norfolk Stakes** (Group 2)<br>Last year's winner: The Ridler 50-1 | **5f** 2yo | £110,000 |
| 3.05 **King George V Stakes** (Handicap)<br>Last year's winner: Secret State 4-1jf | **1m4f** 3yo | £100,000 |
| 3.40 **Ribblesdale Stakes** (Group 2)<br>Last year's winner: Magical Lagoon 11-4 | **1m4f** 3yo fillies | £225,000 |
| 4.20 **Gold Cup** (Group 1)<br>Last year's winner: Kyprios 13-8f | **2m4f** 4yo+ | £600,000 |
| 5.00 **Britannia Stakes** (Heritage Handicap)<br>Last year's winner: Thesis 14-1 | **1m** 3yo<br>colts and geldings | £120,000 |
| 5.35 **Hampton Court Stakes** (Group 3)<br>Last year's winner: Claymore 7-1 | **1m2f** 3yo | £150,000 |
| 6.10 **Buckingham Palace Stakes** (Handicap)<br>Last year's winner: Inver Park 12-1 | **7f** 3yo+ | £100,000 |

Race value is total prize-money

FIRST run in 1843, this is the meeting's third Group 2 race for two-year-olds, following the Coventry and Queen Mary Stakes, and its distinguishing feature is that it is open to both sexes over the minimum distance of five furlongs.

**Last year's winner** Paul Hanagan's winning ride on 50-1 shot The Ridler was highly controversial, with up to four rivals hampered when his mount veered violently left, but the result was allowed to stand on appeal. The winner did not fare badly on key trends but looked fortunate to take the prize.

**Form** Most winners have been pushed hard enough beforehand to achieve an adjusted RPR well into three figures and A'Ali in 2019 is the only maiden to take this

### Key trends
► By a sire with a stamina index between 6.7f and 8.3f, nine winners in last ten runnings
► Lost maiden tag, 9/10
► Top-three finish last time out, 9/10 (seven won)
► Adjusted RPR of at least 100, 7/10

### Other factors
► Four were once-raced

prize since 1990, having been a neck second on his only outing.

**Key races** Most winners have not been highly tried, often running at mid-ranking tracks. Eleven of the last 25 winners had won their only start, with connections happy they had done enough before Ascot (another was unbeaten in three starts).

winners. The other six were all beaten on their debuts
► Only five winners had scored over 5f. Two winners who had yet to score over the trip had won over 4½f and were trained by Wesley Ward
► Seven fillies have run in the last decade, finishing 3990156

**Trainers** Along with the ever-dangerous Aidan O'Brien, trainers known for fast horses have done well, including Richard Fahey with the last two winners.

**Betting** The extent to which connections know what they have on their hands is clear from the fact that only six of the last 25 winners went off bigger than 10-1.

## Story of the last ten years

| | FORM | WINNER | AGE | & WGT | Adj RPR | SP | TRAINER | BEST RPR LAST 12 MONTHS (RUNS SINCE) |
|---|---|---|---|---|---|---|---|---|
| 22 | 413 | **The Ridler** D | 2 | 9-3 | 102-11 | 50-1 | Richard Fahey | 3rd Beverley Class 2 cond (5f) (0) |
| 21 | 31 | **Perfect Power** D | 2 | 9-1 | 94-13 | 14-1 | Richard Fahey | won Hamilton Class 5 maiden (5f) (0) |
| 20 | 1 | **The Lir Jet** D | 2 | 9-1 | 100-3 | 9-2 | Michael Bell | won Yarmouth Class 5 novice (5f) (0) |
| 19 | 2 | **A'Ali** BF | 2 | 9-1 | 101-15 | 5-1 | Simon Crisford | 2nd Ripon Class 5 novice (5f) (0) |
| 18 | 1 | **Shang Shang Shang** | 2 | 8-12 | 99-15 | 5-1 | Wesley Ward (USA) | won Keeneland maiden (4½f) (0) |
| 17 | 3216 | **Sioux Nation** | 2 | 9-1 | 103-10 | 14-1 | Aidan O'Brien (IRE) | won Cork maiden (6f) (1) |
| 16 | 1 | **Prince Of Lir** D | 2 | 9-1 | 105-11 | 8-1 | Robert Cowell | won Beverley Class 2 cond (5f) (0) |
| 15 | 6321 | **Waterloo Bridge** D | 2 | 9-1 | 97-23 | 12-1 | Aidan O'Brien (IRE) | won Tipperary maiden (5f) (0) |
| 14 | 211 | **Baitha Alga** | 2 | 9-1 | 110-2 | 8-1 | Richard Hannon | won Woodcote Stakes Listed (6f) (0) |
| 13 | 1 | **No Nay Never** | 2 | 9-1 | 104-10 | 4-1 | Wesley Ward (USA) | won Keeneland maiden (4½f) (0) |

**FAVOURITES** -£10.00

**TRAINERS IN THIS RACE** (w-pl-r): Aidan O'Brien 2-2-11, Richard Fahey 2-1-8, Wesley Ward 2-1-8, Richard Hannon 1-2-8, Robert Cowell 1-1-6, Michael Bell 1-0-2, William Haggas 0-0-4, Karl Burke 0-1-4, Andrew Balding 0-1-2, Clive Cox 0-0-4

**FATE OF FAVOURITES** 2535200042 **POSITION OF WINNER IN MARKET** 2335932369

# 3.05 King George V Stakes

FIRST run at Royal Ascot in 1948, this is a fascinating yet tricky 1m4f handicap for three-year-olds, open to fillies as well as colts and geldings.

## Last year's winner
Godolphin's Secret State, sent off 4-1 joint-favourite, scored by a head. He was in the ideal ratings band but defied key trends on weight, handicap experience and draw.

**Form** Classy stayer Brown Panther in 2011 and Baghdad in 2018 are the only recent winners who had raced this far before but one clue to potential stamina can be gleaned from two-year-old form. The last winner who had been unraced at two was Heron Bay in 2007 and 13 of the 15 winners since had been tried over 1m-1m2f as juveniles (the other two had run at 7f and 7½f).

**Draw** Eight consecutive winners came from a double-figure stall up to 2018 but three of the last four have been in single figures. A low draw can be tricky but is not such an issue for a prominent racer.

**Key races** Eight winners in the past decade had been racing in handicaps leading up to this test and all but one of them had been successful in that sphere, six of them last time out.

**Trainers** The bigger stables have the strength in depth that gives them a better chance of housing the right type of lightly raced challenger. Two to watch in this and other 1m4f races are Charlie Johnston (father Mark had six winners) and Sir Michael Stoute (four). Godolphin have won four of the past nine runnings (with three different trainers), while Aidan O'Brien has had a winner and a runner-up in two of the last three editions where he had a representative.

**Betting** Since Cosmic Sun scored at 66-1 in 2009, eight of the 13 winners have come from the top four in the betting.

## Key trends
▶ Top-two finish last time, 10/10 (seven won)
▶ Officially rated between 88 and 95, 10/10
▶ Carried no more than 9st 1lb, 8/10
▶ Previously contested a handicap, 7/10 (six won one)
▶ Won earlier in the season, 8/10
▶ Drawn in double figures, 7/10

## Other factors
▶ Mark Johnston has had six winners since 1995, while Sir Michael Stoute has had four

| | FORM | WINNER | AGE & WGT | OR | SP | TRAINER | BEST RPR LAST 12 MONTHS (RUNS SINCE) |
|---|---|---|---|---|---|---|---|
| 22 | 211 | **Secret State** | 3 9-6 | 93T | 4-1j | Charlie Appleby | won Nottingham Class 5 nov (1m½f) (0) |
| 21 | 91-21 | **Surefire** (6ex) | 3 8-9 | 88-2 | 5-1 | Ralph Beckett | won Leicester Class 4 hcap (1m2f) (0) |
| 20 | 21- | **Hukum** | 3 8-11 | 90-9 | 12-1 | Owen Burrows | won Kempton Class 4 novice (1m) (0) |
| 19 | 2-B12 | **South Pacific** (1ow) BF | 3 8-10 | 94-10 | 22-1 | Aidan O'Brien (IRE) | 2nd Naas rated (1m2f) (0) |
| 18 | 41-31 | **Baghdad** D | 3 8-12 | 90-2 | 9-1 | Mark Johnston | won York Class 4 hcap (1m4f) (0) |
| 17 | 1-12 | **Atty Persse** BF | 3 8-7 | 93-2 | 7-1 | Roger Charlton | 2nd Haydock Class 3 hcap (1m2f) (0) |
| 16 | 21-11 | **Gold Mount** | 3 9-3 | 95-3 | 13-2 | Alan King | won Sandown Class 3 hcap (1m2f) (0) |
| 15 | 31-51 | **Space Age** | 3 8-10 | 88T | 9-1 | Charlie Appleby | won Newmarket Class 3 hcap (1m2f) (0) |
| 14 | 1-31 | **Elite Army** | 3 9-1 | 94-5 | 4-1j | Saeed bin Suroor | won Sandown Class 3 hcap (1m2f) (0) |
| 13 | 4-322 | **Elidor** | 3 9-0 | 88-5 | 20-1 | Mick Channon | 2nd Lingfield Listed (1m3½f) (0) |

**FAVOURITES** -£5.50 **FATE OF FAVOURITES:** 3100000221 **POSITION OF WINNER IN MARKET:** 0143250821

51

FIRST run in 1919, this 1m4f highlight is the meeting's premier race for middle-distance fillies from the Classic generation and often draws runners who have competed in the Oaks or at least the trials.

## Last year's winner

Magical Lagoon had been competing in good class and became the first RPR top-rated to win since 2011 but didn't hit the key trends on winning form either recently or beyond a mile. She went on to land the Group 1 Irish Oaks next time out.

**Form** If you removed Group 1 runs that season from the records of the winners since 2010, they would show 14 wins, three seconds and four thirds from 22 runs. That clearly points towards a

### Key trends

▸ *Raced no more than three times at two, 10/10*
▸ *Adjusted RPR of at least 111, 9/10*
▸ *Contested a Listed or Group race, 8/10 (three had won a Group race)*
▸ *Won one of last two starts, 7/10*
▸ *Won over at least 1m2f, 6/10*

high-performing filly who has been just short of Group 1 standard.

**Key races** Five winners since 2010 had run in a Guineas or the Oaks, although none finished closer than fourth and that explains why they were going for this Group 2 rather than a top-level target. A placing in a minor Oaks or a trial is often a significant marker.

### Other factors

▸ *Last year Magical Lagoon was the first RPR top-rated winner since Banimpire in 2011. The other nine were between 5lb and 16lb off top*
▸ *Four winners failed to shed their maiden tag the previous season, while another did not run as a juvenile*

**Trainers** In the past 17 runnings the winner has come from Newmarket (ten) or Irish yards (seven) and in particular the Gosden stable and Aidan O'Brien have exerted their influence with seven of the last nine winners between them.

**Betting** Only one of the last 16 winners was outside the top five in the market, with ten of them in the top two.

## Story of the last ten years

| | FORM | WINNER | AGE & WGT | Adj RPR | SP | TRAINER | BEST RPR LAST 12 MONTHS (RUNS SINCE) |
|---|---|---|---|---|---|---|---|
| 22 | 417-2 | **Magical Lagoon** | 3 9-2 | 119$^T$ | 11-4 | Jessica Harrington (IRE) | 2nd Navan Listed (1m2f) (0) |
| 21 | 71-25 | **Loving Dream** | 3 9-0 | 111-14 | 18-1 | John & Thady Gosden | 2nd Wetherby Class 5 maiden (1m2f) (1) |
| 20 | 2-1 | **Frankly Darling** | 3 9-0 | 109-8 | 11-8f | John Gosden | won Newcastle Class 5 maiden (1m2f) (0) |
| 19 | 6-13 | **Star Catcher** | 3 9-0 | 113-13 | 4-1 | John Gosden | 3rd Newbury Fillies' Trial (1m2f) (0) |
| 18 | 7-314 | **Magic Wand** | 3 9-0 | 120-5 | 10-3 | Aidan O'Brien (IRE) | won Cheshire Oaks Gp3 (1m3½f) (1) |
| 17 | 11-35 | **Coronet** | 3 9-0 | 114-9 | 9-1 | John Gosden | 3rd Prix Saint-Alary Gp1 (1m2f) (1) |
| 16 | 31-3 | **Even Song** | 3 9-0 | 113-16 | 15-8f | Aidan O'Brien (IRE) | 3rd Newmarket Listed (1m2f) (0) |
| 15 | 8-111 | **Curvy** | 3 9-0 | 122-5 | 9-2 | David Wachman (IRE) | won Curragh Gp3 (1m2f) (0) |
| 14 | 81-10 | **Bracelet** | 3 9-0 | 119-7 | 10-1 | Aidan O'Brien (IRE) | won Leopardstown Gp3 (7f) (1) |
| 13 | 21 | **Riposte** D | 3 8-12 | 111-14 | 9-2 | Lady Cecil | 2nd Sandown Class 4 maiden (1m2f) (1) |

**FAVOURITES:** -£4.75

**TRAINERS IN THIS RACE** (w-pl-r) Aidan O'Brien 3-4-16, John & Thady Gosden 1-0-3, Charlie Appleby 0-1-2, Jessica Harrington 1-0-1, Richard Hannon 0-1-2, Ralph Beckett 0-0-6, Roger Varian 0-2-6, Sir Michael Stoute 0-3-8, William Haggas 0-1-6

**FATE OF FAVOURITES:** 4421222162 **POSITION OF WINNER IN MARKET:** 2521432182

# IRISH CHAMPIONS FESTIVAL

Leopardstown and The Curragh
on 9th & 10th September 2023

2 incredible days of world-class racing and entertainment

IT ALL COMES DOWN TO THIS

Early Bird tickets on sale now at **ChampionsFestival.ie**

# 4.20 Gold Cup

FOUNDED in 1807, this is one of the crown jewels of Royal Ascot and at two and a half miles is the premier staying race of the British Flat season.

**Last year's winner**
Kyprios won by half a length as 13-8 favourite, with hat-trick hero Stradivarius a somewhat unlucky third. The Aidan O'Brien-trained winner scored well on trends, although he had yet to win over further than 1m6f.

**Form** The class factor is important, with 20 of the 23 winners since 2000 having previously struck in a Group 1 or Group 2 (15 had won at the highest level). Only follow-up winners Royal Rebel, Yeats and Stradivarius, along with 2005 winner Westerner, had scored at this trip before, but just four (all trained by O'Brien) had yet to win over at least 2m.

**Key races** There is not a wide choice of targets for stayers and almost every recent winner has come down the Sagaro/Henry II/ Yorkshire Cup route in Britain or via the Vintage Crop/Saval Beg in Ireland. Ten of the last 16 winners had won at least one of those

The Ascot Gold Cup, a coveted prize that dates back to 1807

races en route (Kyprios last year won both Irish races) and another had been runner-up in the Henry II. The previous year's Gold Cup is also a guide – ten horses have won the race more than once in the near half-century since Sagaro, one of the greats, started his hat-trick in 1975.

**Trainers** O'Brien has been the dominant force in recent years. He has won eight of the last 17 runnings with five different horses. His only multiple scorer is Yeats, who is still out on his own as a four-time winner (2006-2009).

**Betting** Fancied runners have an excellent record. Only three of the 23 winners since 2000 were outside the top four in the market and 16 were in the top two.

## Key trends

▶ *Sire stamina index in excess of 9.5f, 10/10*
▶ *Won within last two starts, 9/10*
▶ *Adjusted RPR of at least 126, 9/10*
▶ *Group-race winner, 9/10 (six had won a Group 1)*
▶ *Won over at least 2m, 8/10*
▶ *Rated within 5lb of RPR top-rated, 8/10 (four were top-rated)*

## Other factors

▶ *Eight winners were competing in the race for the first time (Stradivarius in 2019 and 2020 accounts for both exceptions)*
▶ *Winners of the Sagaro Stakes finished 172732246*
▶ *Seven favourites have won in the last decade (including one joint-favourite) but Stradivarius*

*was the only one to have previously scored over the trip*

## Roll of honour

**Longest-priced winner**
25-1 Indian Queen (1991)

**Shortest-priced winner**
1-5 Ardross (1981)

**Most successful trainer**
8 wins: **Aidan O'Brien**
Yeats (2006, 2007, 2008, 2009), Fame And Glory (2011), Leading Light (2014), Order Of St George (2016), Kyprios (2022)

**Most successful jockey**
11 wins: **Lester Piggott**
Zarathustra (1957), Gladness (1958), Pandofell (1961), Twilight Alley (1963), Fighting Charlie (1965), Sagaro (1975, 1976, 1977), Le Moss (1979), Ardross (1981, 1982)

**Most successful owner**
7 wins: **Coolmore partners**
Yeats (2006, 2007, 2008, 2009), Fame And Glory (2011), Leading Light (2014), Order Of St George (2016)

*All figures since 1946

### Story of the last ten years

| | FORM | WINNER | AGE | & WGT | Adj RPR | SP | TRAINER | BEST RPR LAST 12 MONTHS (RUNS SINCE) |
|---|---|---|---|---|---|---|---|---|
| 22 | 14-11 | **Kyprios** | 4 | 9-3 | 130$^{-2}$ | 13-8f | Aidan O'Brien (IRE) | won Saval Beg Gp3 (1m6f) (0) |
| 21 | 171-1 | **Subjectivist** | 4 | 9-1 | 127$^{-10}$ | 13-2 | Mark Johnston | won Dubai Gold Cup Gp2 (2m) (0) |
| 20 | 112-3 | **Stradivarius** CD | 6 | 9-2 | 135$^{T}$ | 4-5f | John Gosden | won Goodwood Cup Gp1 (2m) (4) |
| 19 | 111-1 | **Stradivarius** CD | 5 | 9-2 | 133$^{T}$ | Evsf | John Gosden | won Goodwood Cup Gp1 (2m) (3) |
| 18 | 133-1 | **Stradivarius** C | 4 | 9-1 | 132$^{-5}$ | 7-4j | John Gosden | 3rd St Leger Gp1 (1m6½f) (2) |
| 17 | 30-41 | **Big Orange** C | 6 | 9-2 | 131$^{-3}$ | 5-1 | Michael Bell | won Princess of Wales's Gp2 (1m4f) (6) |
| 16 | 111-1 | **Order Of St George** | 4 | 9-0 | 137$^{T}$ | 10-11f | Aidan O'Brien (IRE) | won Irish St Leger Gp1 (1m6f) (1) |
| 15 | 41112 | **Trip To Paris** C | 4 | 9-0 | 121$^{-10}$ | 12-1 | Ed Dunlop | 2nd Henry II Stakes Gp3 (2m) (0) |
| 14 | 110-1 | **Leading Light** C | 4 | 9-0 | 133$^{T}$ | 10-11f | Aidan O'Brien (IRE) | won Vintage Crop Stakes Gp3 (1m6f) (0) |
| 13 | 133-1 | **Estimate** C | 4 | 8-11 | 126$^{-4}$ | 7-2f | Sir Michael Stoute | won Sagaro Stakes Gp3 (2m) (0) |

**WINS-RUNS** 4yo 7-7-46, 5yo 1-5-28, 6yo+ 2-8-45 **FAVOURITES** £6.12

**TRAINERS IN THIS RACE** Aidan O'Brien 3-2-13, Andrew Balding 0-1-6, Brian Ellison 0-0-1, Charlie Appleby 0-1-4, Willie Mullins 0-1-7, Ralph Beckett 0-0-3, Joseph O'Brien 0-1-2, John & Thady Gosden 0-1-2

**FATE OF FAVOURITES** 1131211141 **POSITION OF WINNER IN MARKET** 1161211121

FIRST run in 1928, this contest over the straight mile is the second of Royal Ascot's three heritage handicaps and is open to three-year-old colts and geldings.

**Last year's winner** Thesis had yet to win or compete outside novice/maiden company but was in the right ratings and weight range and got first run on royal challenger Saga to score at 14-1 for the training partnership of Harry and Roger Charlton (a first Royal Ascot winner for Harry and the 11th for his father).

**Form** A good level of form is important, with Thesis last year in the top six on Racing Post Ratings. Most winners have been lightly raced, with seven of the last ten having had no more than four outings. Getting in on a weight just below 9st might

### Key trends

▶ *At least one top-three finish within last two starts, 9/10*

▶ *Officially rated between 90 and 99, 8/10*

▶ *Won in current season over 7f or a mile, 7/10*

▶ *Carried no more than 9st 1lb, 7/10*

▶ *Rated within 6lb of RPR top-rated, 7/10*

▶ *Previously contested a handicap, 6/10 (four had won one)*

### Other factors

▶ *Four winners had won a handicap, while another four were making their handicap debut*

▶ *The Gosden yard hasn't won this for a while but was successful four times between 1996 and 2001*

be ideal, with 13 of the last 20 winners having been in the range from 8st 8lb to 8st 13lb.

**Draw** Six of the last ten winners have been in the middle third (stalls 11-20) and only one was lower than that. An experienced, tactically astute jockey is an advantage. Seven of the last eight runnings have gone to a rider with a championship on their CV.

**Key races** Most winners had been restricted to maiden, novice and latterly handicap company, with six winners in the past decade having run in a handicap before coming here (four had won a handicap).

**Trainers** The only repeat winner in the last 20 runnings is Roger Charlton (successful with Fifteen Love in 2008 and in partnership with son Harry last year).

**Betting** Six winners in the past decade were sent off at 14-1 or bigger and there has been only one successful favourite since 2006.

## Story of the last ten years

| | FORM | WINNER | AGE & WGT | OR | SP | TRAINER | BEST RPR LAST 12 MONTHS (RUNS SINCE) |
|---|---|---|---|---|---|---|---|
| 22 | 3-222 | **Thesis** BF | 3 8-11 | 90-5 | 14-1 | Harry & Roger Charlton | 2nd Doncaster Class 5 novice (7f) (0) |
| 21 | 3-241 | **Perotto** (5ex) | 3 9-3 | 99-8 | 18-1 | Marcus Tregoning | 2nd Newmarket Class 2 hcap (6f) (2) |
| 20 | 21 | **Khaloosy** | 3 9-2 | 94-17 | 9-2 | Roger Varian | won Wolves Class 5 novice (1m½f) (0) |
| 19 | 112 | **Biometric** BF | 3 8-8 | 92-7 | 28-1 | Ralph Beckett | won Newbury Class 4 novice (7f) (1) |
| 18 | 2-221 | **Ostilio** D | 3 8-9 | 90-3 | 10-1 | Simon Crisford | won Newmarket Class 4 hcap (1m)(0) |
| 17 | 2135 | **Bless Him** D | 3 8-9 | 90-6 | 25-1 | David Simcock | 5th Goodwood Class 2 hcap (7f) (0) |
| 16 | 3-141 | **Limitless** D | 3 9-1 | 95T | 13-2 | Jamie Osborne | won Doncaster Class 4 hcap (1m) (0) |
| 15 | -2470 | **War Envoy** | 3 9-6 | 104T | 10-1 | Aidan O'Brien (IRE) | 5th Prix Jean-Luc Lagardere Gp1 (7f) (5) |
| 14 | 312 | **Born In China** D | 3 8-4 | 87-1 | 14-1 | Andrew Balding | 2nd Newmarket Class 2 hcap (1m) (0) |
| 13 | 01-41 | **Beauty Flame** D | 3 8-12 | 96-6 | 20-1 | Joanna Morgan (IRE) | won Curragh hcap (1m) (0) |

**FAVOURITES** -£10.00

**FATE OF FAVOURITES** 4406002290 **POSITION OF WINNER IN MARKET** 8643050277

At **Ascot Top Hats Ltd**, we provide new felt Toppers and Vintage Silk Top Hats, as well as refurbishment and fitting services to reshape hats to heads to make them comfortable.

## Ascot Top Hats Ltd

By appointment at our workshop please call:
**01344 638 838 www.ascot-tophats.co.uk**

Unit 24 Space Business Centre,
Molly Millars Lane, Wokingham, Berks RG41 2PQ

**Ascot Top Hats Ltd is a company registered in England and Wales
Incorporation Number: 5740259 Registered Office: Beechey House,
87 Church Street, Crowthorne, Berkshire, RG45 7AW**

# 5.35 Hampton Court Stakes

THIS Group 3 race for three-year-olds was added to the programme when Royal Ascot was extended to five days in 2002 and upgraded to its current level in 2011.

**Last year's winner** Reach For The Moon was hot favourite at 2-5 in a field of six but appeared to be outstayed by front-runner Claymore (7-1 second favourite), who missed most of the key trends but had been competing at a high level.

**Form** Five of the 21 winners since 2002 were unraced as two-year-olds and another six had failed to win at that age. A last-time-out success is a good pointer, although failure to win can be more readily excused if that run was in a Classic or another Group 1.

## Key trends

▶ Yet to win at this level or higher, 10/10
▶ Adjusted RPR of at least 120, 9/10
▶ Rated within 6lb of RPR top-rated, 8/10 (five were top-rated)
▶ Won that season, 8/10
▶ Top-three finish last time out, 7/10 (five won)
▶ Distance winner, 6/10

## Other factors

▶ Three had won a handicap that season
▶ Five had been beaten in Classic trials

**Key races** There are two main routes to this race – either through handicaps (three of the last ten winners) or from the Classic trail. In 2020 Russian Emperor was en route to the Derby (run after Royal Ascot that year), where he was seventh, while in 2021 Mohaafeth came here after being a Derby non-runner due to the ground. Last year Claymore had been second in the Craven Stakes before finishing last from a poor draw in the French 2,000 Guineas.

**Trainers** The roll of honour is dominated by the big yards that house plenty of later-developing three-year-olds, with nine of the last ten winners having come from Newmarket or Aidan O'Brien's Ballydoyle stable. O'Brien had the third in 2016, the second and fourth in 2017, the winner in 2018 and 2020 and the runner-up in 2021.

**Betting** Most winners had done enough to take high rank in the betting, with eight of the last ten coming from the top two and none of the ten bigger than 7-1.

## Story of the last ten years

| | FORM | WINNER | AGE & WGT | Adj RPR | SP | TRAINER | BEST RPR LAST 12 MONTHS (RUNS SINCE) |
|---|---|---|---|---|---|---|---|
| 22 | 1-20 | **Claymore** | 3 9-2 | 121-8 | 7-1 | Jane Chapple-Hyam | 2nd Craven Gp3 (1m) (1) |
| 21 | 3-111 | **Mohaafeth** D | 3 9-0 | 131T | 11-8f | William Haggas | won Newmarket Listed (1m2f) (0) |
| 20 | 3-12 | **Russian Emperor** BF | 3 9-0 | 98-28 | 10-3 | Aidan O'Brien (IRE) | 2nd Leopardstown Gp3 (1m2f) (0) |
| 19 | 114-3 | **Sangarius** | 3 9-0 | 120-6 | 13-2 | Sir Michael Stoute | 3rd Sandown Listed (1m) (0) |
| 18 | -1336 | **Hunting Horn** D | 3 9-0 | 124T | 5-1 | Aidan O'Brien (IRE) | 6th Prix du Jockey Club Gp1 (1m2½f) (0) |
| 17 | 1325 | **Benbatl** | 3 9-0 | 128T | 9-2 | Saeed bin Suroor | 5th Derby Gp1 (1m4f) (0) |
| 16 | 111-1 | **Hawkbill** D | 3 9-0 | 121-4 | 11-2 | Charlie Appleby | won Newmarket Listed (1m2f) (0) |
| 15 | 212-1 | **Time Test** D | 3 9-0 | 123T | 15-8f | Roger Charlton | won Newbury Class 2 hcap (1m2f) (0) |
| 14 | 2-11 | **Cannock Chase** D | 3 9-0 | 122-1 | 7-4f | Sir Michael Stoute | won Newbury Class 2 hcap (1m2f) (0) |
| 13 | 311 | **Remote** D | 3 9-0 | 127T | 9-4f | John Gosden | won Doncaster Class 2 hcap (1m) (0) |

**FAVOURITES** £1.25

**TRAINERS IN THIS RACE** (w-pl-r) Sir Michael Stoute 2-3-8, Aidan O'Brien 2-3-13, Saeed bin Suroor 1-1-7, Charlie Appleby 1-1-6, William Haggas 1-1-2, Jane Chapple-Hyam 1-0-1, Roger Varian 0-0-4, John & Thady Gosden 0-1-1, Ralph Beckett 0-0-1

**FATE OF FAVOURITES** 1112262212 **POSITION OF WINNER IN MARKET** 1114224212

ORIGINALLY introduced to the expanded royal meeting in 2002, this big-field seven-furlong handicap for three-year-olds and upwards was removed after 2014 to make room for the new Group 1 Commonwealth Cup but reinstated in 2020 as part of the extended race programme.

**Last year's winner** Inver Park won at 12-1 to give Newmarket trainer George Boughey his first Royal Ascot success (he added a second later in the meeting with Missed The Cut in the Golden Gates Handicap). The four-year-old was on the up, completing a hat-trick here, but bucked a couple of key trends as this was his first try at Class 2 or in a big field.

**Form** This favours a progressive type who gets in on a mid-range weight. In the three runnings since the race's resumption, all bar one of the first three places have gone to a four-year-old.

## Key trends
▶ *At least one top-three finish within last three starts 5/5*
▶ *Officially rated 92 to 99, 5/5*
▶ *Carried no more than 9st 4lb, 5/5*
▶ *Winner at Class 2 level at least, 3/5*
▶ *Aged four or five, 4/5*
▶ *Won or placed in a handicap with at least 19 runners, 3/5*

## Other factors
▶ *Two winners had yet to score at the trip*
▶ *All five winners were priced between 12-1 and 33-1*

Good form in a big-field handicap is a positive pointer.

**Draw** A high draw is often an advantage, although Inver Park bucked the trend last year from stall two. The previous four winners had come from stalls 32, 29, 26 and 31.

**Key races** The Victoria Cup over the same course and distance in May is an obvious stepping stone (last used successfully by Louis The Pious in 2014). Recent 7f/1m handicaps at Newmarket, Haydock and York are worth checking.

**Trainers** The only trainer to have won more than once is Kevin Ryan with Uhoomagoo (2006) and Lightning Cloud (2013).

**Betting** There has never been a successful favourite in the 16 runnings and the only winners not at double-figure odds were 8-1 shots Unscrupulous (2004) and Jedburgh (2005).

Inver Park heads to victory in last year's race

## Story of recent years

| | FORM | WINNER | AGE & WGT | OR | SP | TRAINER | BEST RPR LAST 12 MONTHS (RUNS SINCE) |
|---|---|---|---|---|---|---|---|
| 22 | -2311 | **Inver Park** C | 4 9-1 | 94-2 | 12-1 | George Boughey | won Hamilton Class 4 handicap (6f) (0) |
| 21 | 0-312 | **Highfield Princess** D, BF | 4 8-11 | 92-3 | 18-1 | John Quinn | won Haydock Class 4 handicap (7f) (1) |
| 20 | 1216- | **Motakhayyel** D | 4 9-3 | 98-6 | 14-1 | Richard Hannon | won Newmarket Class 2 handicap (1m) (1) |
| 14 | 9-720 | **Louis The Pious** | 6 9-4 | 99-4 | 33-1 | David O'Meara | 2nd Haydock Class 2 handicap (7f) (1) |
| 13 | 3-307 | **Lightning Cloud** CD | 5 8-13 | 93-1 | 25-1 | Kevin Ryan | 3rd Ascot Class 2 app handicap (7f) (3) |

**WINS-RUNS** 3yo 0-0-1, 4yo 3-9-58, 5yo 1-3-34, 6yo+ 1-3-42 **FAVOURITES** -£5.00

**FATE OF FAVOURITES:** 00055 **POSITION OF WINNER IN MARKET:** 00686

Racing Post Ratings handicapper Matt Gardner picks six horses with the form and potential to make their mark at Royal Ascot

### ELDAR ELDAROV
**4yo colt**
**Trainer: Roger Varian**
**RPR 119**

The absence of Kyprios throws the Gold Cup wide open and Eldar Eldarov could be the one to take advantage. His progressive three-year-old campaign included victory at this meeting in the Queen's Vase before landing the St Leger. Although disappointing when upped to two miles for the first time in the Long Distance Cup, that possibly came too soon after his Doncaster exertions, and he returned this year with a fine second in the Yorkshire Cup. Still low-mileage after just seven starts, he appeals as the sort who could have plenty more to offer.

### MIDNIGHT AFFAIR
**2yo filly**
**Richard Fahey**
**RPR 90**

Soprano may be higher up the betting for the Albany but the filly who finished second to her on their Newmarket debuts is of more interest. A sister to Rhythm Master, Midnight Affair was unfortunate not to emerge on top that day having met plenty of trouble, something especially noteworthy as her yard's juveniles have generally needed the experience of a first run this year. She's open to significant improvement and is likely to stay six furlongs, although connections also have the option of the Queen Mary, which her owner won last year with Dramatised.

### NOBLE STYLE
**3yo colt**
**Charlie Appleby**
**RPR 119**

Noble Style was one of the most talented juveniles last year with an RPR surpassed only by Little Big Bear and Auguste Rodin. It's easy to see why connections tried to stretch him out for the 2,000 Guineas, with Godolphin light in that department compared to Derby prospects, but he was far too keen and on pedigree and run style he's all over a sprinter. The Commonwealth Cup looks tailor-made for him and his RPR is already good enough to have seen him win five of the eight runnings.

## ORAZIO
**4yo colt**
**Charlie Hills**
**RPR 114**

Orazio was a decent juvenile in 2021 but, having missed 2022, he's taken his form to a whole new level this year, looking one of the most progressive sprinters around. His win at the Craven meeting has proved to be strong form, with the next three going on to finish first, second and fourth when they met again at the Guineas meeting, and Orazio followed up with another impressive success at Ascot. That match practice over the Wokingham course and distance will stand him in excellent stead for the big sprint handicap and he still looks well treated from a new handicap mark of 101.

## RIVER TIBER
**2yo colt**
**Aidan O'Brien**
**RPR 104**

It's rare for a juvenile to achieve a three-figure RPR on debut (it happened just six times last year) and rarer still for it to be done quite so early in the season as River Tiber managed. It was an expression of ability not to be overlooked. His ten-length win at Navan on April 22 rocketed him to the head of the Coventry betting and he holds excellent claims of giving his trainer a remarkable tenth win in the race.

## TAHIYRA
**3yo filly**
**Dermot Weld**
**RPR 117**

Tahiyra, last year's highest-rated juvenile filly, may have been beaten at a short price in the 1,000 Guineas but she emerged with her reputation enhanced. Pulling more than seven lengths clear of the third, Tahiyra did everything right but found her lack of experience relative to Mawj costing her in a battling finish, with that rival also having a fitness edge after being campaigned in Dubai during the winter. Tahiyra remains an exciting prospect who looks capable of reversing the form with Mawj if they meet again in the Coronation.

> **66** Orazio was a decent juvenile in 2021 but, having missed 2022, he's taken his form to a whole new level **99**

Tahiyra (nearside): can reverse 1,000 Guineas form with Mawj

# DAY FOUR

The Coronation Stakes remains the traditional Friday centrepiece but the recent addition of the Commonwealth Cup has introduced another highlight to a sparkling card. After Tuesday's opening salvo, this is the only other day with more than one Group 1 contest.

The Coronation Stakes, over a mile for three-year-old fillies, often attracts graduates from the 1,000 Guineas, Irish 1,000 Guineas and Poule d'Essai des Pouliches in a clash that can sort out the Classic form.

Last year brought together the Guineas winners from Britain (Cachet) and France (Mangoustine), who had already met at Longchamp, as well as a pair of high-class American raiders. However, they were no match for Inspiral, who had been longtime ante-post favourite for the Newmarket Classic but had to miss the race after a setback.

The Commonwealth Cup, introduced in 2015, has been quick to establish a high standing as an early top-level opportunity for three-year-old sprinters without having to take on their elders.

The first running was won by champion sprinter Muhaarar and the latest went to Perfect Power, whose class was well established after a pair of Group 1 wins as a juvenile.

Classic form is also on show in the King Edward VII Stakes, the only Group 2 on the card. Often called the Ascot Derby, this mile-and-a-half race regularly attracts horses who have participated in the premier Classic at Epsom.

Friday's programme begins with the Group 3 Albany Stakes, the first of three races on the day restricted to fillies. The past two runnings of this six-furlong juvenile contest have featured Cachet (fifth in 2021) and Mawj

(runner-up last year), who both went on to claim 1,000 Guineas glory the next spring.

The first handicap on the card is the Duke of Edinburgh Stakes for three-year-olds and up over a mile and a half. Later comes the Sandringham Stakes, a hotly contested handicap for three-year-old fillies over the straight mile, and the card is completed by the Palace of Holyroodhouse Stakes, a five-furlong handicap for three-year-olds.

# Friday June 23

2.30 **Albany Stakes** (Group 3)  **6f** 2yo fillies  £100,000
Last year's winner: Meditate 5-2

3.05 **Commonwealth Cup** (Group 1)  **6f** 3yo  £600,000
Last year's winner: Perfect Power 7-2jf  colts and fillies

3.40 **Duke of Edinburgh Stakes** (Handicap)  **1m4f** 3yo+  £100,000
Last year's winner: Candleford 11-2

4.20 **Coronation Stakes** (Group 1)  **1m** 3yo fillies  £600,000
Last year's winner: Inspiral 15-8f

5.00 **Sandringham Stakes** (Handicap)  **1m** 3yo fillies  £100,000
Last year's winner: Heredia 7-2f

5.35 **King Edward VII Stakes** (Group 2)  **1m4f** 3yo  £250,000
Last year's winner: Changingoftheguard 11-10f  colts and geldings

6.10 **Palace of Holyroodhouse Stakes** (H'cap)  **5f** 3yo  £100,000
Last year's winner: Latin Lover 5-1

Race value is total prize-money

ESTABLISHED in 2002 at Listed level and upgraded in 2005, this Group 3 6f contest is a two-year-old fillies' version of the Coventry Stakes, albeit without such a long and illustrious history.

## Last year's winner

Meditate was lightly raced, having won both previous starts, but not a typical fit on trends as her form was already at a high level. A Group 3 winner and top-rated on Racing Post Ratings, she overturned favourite Mawj (who has gone on to be this year's 1,000 Guineas winner with Meditate sixth) by a length and three-quarters.

**Form** All of the last ten winners had won at least once (five came here after just one run) and an adjusted

## Key trends

▶ *No more than two runs, ten winners in last ten runnings*
▶ *At least 7lb off top-rated, 9/10 (exception was top-rated)*
▶ *Drawn 13 or higher, 8/10 (last two winners the exceptions)*
▶ *Adjusted Racing Post Rating of at least 98, 8/10*
▶ *Distance winner, 8/10*
▶ *Ran in maiden/novice company last time out, 7/10*
▶ *By a sire with a stamina index of at least 7.4f, 7/10*

## Other factors

▶ *All of the last ten winners had scored last time out. The last maiden to succeed was Samitar in 2011*

RPR of at least 96 has been essential during that period.

**Key races** Victory in a Newmarket and Goodwood maiden/novice is a good sign and three of the last ten winners were once-raced all-weather scorers. Winning a Curragh maiden tends to be the first step for an Irish challenger.

**Trainers** The only trainers with more than one winner in the past decade are Roger Varian and Aidan O'Brien. Former trainer Mick Channon holds the record with three wins in the first ten runnings.

**Betting** This has not been a great race for favourites. Since Cuis Ghaire won at 8-11 in 2008, only three market leaders have been successful. Four of the last ten winners were returned at odds of 14-1 or bigger.

### Story of the last ten years

| FORM | | WINNER | AGE & WGT | Adj RPR | SP | TRAINER | BEST RPR LAST 12 MONTHS (RUNS SINCE) |
|---|---|---|---|---|---|---|---|
| 22 | 11 | **Meditate** D | 2 9-2 | 110T | 5-2 | Aidan O'Brien (IRE) | won Naas Gp3 (6f) (0) |
| 21 | 1 | **Sandrine** D | 2 9-0 | 102-8 | 16-1 | Andrew Balding | won Kempton Class 5 novice (5f) (0) |
| 20 | 1 | **Dandalla** | 2 9-0 | 96-7 | 13-2 | Karl Burke | won Newcastle Class 5 maiden (5f) (0) |
| 19 | 1 | **Daahyeh** D | 2 9-0 | 105-7 | 4-1f | Roger Varian | won Newmarket Class 4 novice (6f) (0) |
| 18 | 11 | **Main Edition** D | 2 9-0 | 104-7 | 7-1 | Mark Johnston | won Goodwood Class 5 novice (6f) (0) |
| 17 | 11 | **Different League** D | 2 9-0 | 96-18 | 20-1 | Matthieu Palussiere (FR) | won Angers conditions stakes (6f) (0) |
| 16 | 81 | **Brave Anna** D | 2 9-0 | 103-14 | 16-1 | Aidan O'Brien (IRE) | won Curragh maiden (6f) (0) |
| 15 | 1 | **Illuminate** | 2 9-0 | 98-12 | 4-1f | Richard Hannon | won Salisbury Class 3 cond (5f) (0) |
| 14 | 1 | **Cursory Glance** D | 2 9-0 | 98-10 | 14-1 | Roger Varian | won Kempton Class 5 maiden (6f) (0) |
| 13 | 41 | **Kiyoshi** D | 2 8-12 | 106-15 | 8-1 | Charlie Hills | won Goodwood Class 5 maiden (6f) (0) |

**FAVOURITES** £0.00

**TRAINERS IN THIS RACE** (w-pl-r) Roger Varian 2-1-6, Aidan O'Brien 2-2-13, Richard Hannon 1-0-10, Andrew Balding 1-0-1, Karl Burke 1-0-2, Charlie Hills 1-0-4, John & Thady Gosden 0-0-2, Wesley Ward 0-1-10, Charlie Appleby 0-1-4

**FATE OF FAVOURITES** 2315201202 **POSITION OF WINNER IN MARKET** 3717931492

# DAY FOUR

THIS 6f sprint for three-year-olds was introduced in 2015 with the aim of allowing them to compete at the top level against their contemporaries without having to take on older horses at such an early stage of the season.

**Last year's winner** Perfect Power was an excellent fit on trends and made a successful drop back in trip after finishing seventh in the 2,000 Guineas, scoring well by a length and a quarter.

**Form** Most winners had plenty of solid form in Group company – in one or more two-year-old races over 5f and 6f, or in that year's early sprints. As a result of their achievements before Royal Ascot, all bar one of the eight winners were no more than 3lb off the top on RPR (the adjusted figure for those seven was at least 128).

**Key races** Inaugural winner Muhaarar set the standard, having landed the Group 2 Gimcrack Stakes at York during his two-year-old career before taking the Group 3 Greenham Stakes on his reappearance at three. The Prix Morny, Middle Park, Dewhurst and Cornwallis Stakes have featured on the CVs of other winners. Perfect Power had won the Morny and Middle Park, as well as Royal Ascot's Norfolk Stakes, at two and

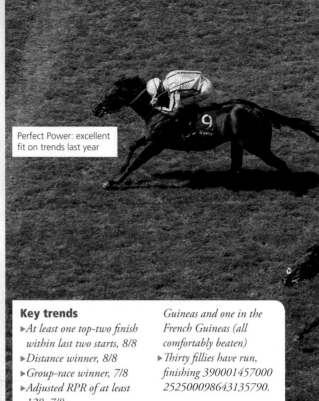

Perfect Power: excellent fit on trends last year

## Key trends
▶ At least one top-two finish within last two starts, 8/8
▶ Distance winner, 8/8
▶ Group-race winner, 7/8
▶ Adjusted RPR of at least 128, 7/8
▶ Rated within 3lb of RPR top-rated, 7/8 (three top-rated)
▶ Top-three finish at the track, 6/8

## Other factors
▶ Three winners contested the Coventry the previous season, finishing 125. One had won the Queen Mary, while another landed the Norfolk
▶ Two had run in the 2,000 Guineas and one in the French Guineas (all comfortably beaten)
▶ Thirty fillies have run, finishing 390001457000 252500098643135790.

## Roll of honour
**Longest-priced winner**
12-1 Eqtidaar (2018)

**Shortest-priced winner**
5-6 Caravaggio (2017)

**Most successful trainer**
No multiple winners

**Most successful jockey**
2 wins: **Frankie Dettori**
Advertise (2019), Campanelle (2021)

**Most successful owner**
2 wins: **Hamdan Al Maktoum**
Muhaarar (2015), Eqtidaar (2018)

*All figures since 2015

then the Greenham first time out at three.

**Trainers** No trainer has won more than once, but it is no surprise to see the names of Charlie Hills, Karl Burke, Clive Cox, Wesley Ward and Richard Fahey (all adept with sprinters) on the roll of honour.

**Betting** Fancied horses have done well, with five of the eight winners coming from the top three in the market.

## Story of the last eight years

| | FORM | WINNER | AGE & WGT | Adj RPR | SP | TRAINER | BEST RPR LAST 12 MONTHS (RUNS SINCE) |
|---|---|---|---|---|---|---|---|
| 22 | 11-17 | **Perfect Power** C, D | 3 9-2 | 130ᵀ | 7-2j | Richard Fahey | won Prix Morny Gp1 (6f) (3) |
| 21 | 1114- | **Campanelle** C, D | 3 8-11 | 131⁻¹ | 5-1 | Wesley Ward (USA) | won Prix Morny Gp1 (6f) (1) |
| 20 | 5132- | **Golden Horde** D | 3 9-0 | 130⁻³ | 5-1 | Clive Cox | 2nd Middle Park Gp1 (6f) (0) |
| 19 | 112-0 | **Advertise** D | 3 9-3 | 128⁻³ | 8-1 | Martyn Meade | 2nd Dewhurst Gp1 (7f) (1) |
| 18 | 14-24 | **Eqtidaar** D | 3 9-3 | 118⁻⁹ | 12-1 | Sir Michael Stoute | 2nd Pavilion Gp3 (6f) (1) |
| 17 | 111-1 | **Caravaggio** CD | 3 9-3 | 131ᵀ | 5-6f | Aidan O'Brien (IRE) | won Lacken Gp3 (6f) (0) |
| 16 | 11-11 | **Quiet Reflection** D | 3 9-0 | 130ᵀ | 7-4f | Karl Burke | won Sandy Lane Gp2 (6f) (0) |
| 15 | 13-18 | **Muhaarar** D | 3 9-3 | 128⁻³ | 10-1 | Charlie Hills | won Greenham Stakes Gp3 (7f) (1) |

**FAVOURITES** -£1.17

**TRAINERS IN THIS RACE** (w-pl-r) Aidan O'Brien 1-1-14, Karl Burke 1-0-5, Charlie Hills 1-0-5, Clive Cox 1-1-8, Wesley Ward 1-1-4, Richard Fahey 1-2-4, Charlie Appleby 0-1-4, Archie Watson 0-1-2, Kevin Ryan 0-1-5, Richard Hannon 0-0-8, Roger Varian 0-0-4

**FATE OF FAVOURITES** 01104001 **POSITION OF WINNER IN MARKET** 61155331

# DAY FOUR  3.40 Duke of Edinburgh Stakes

THIS prestigious and valuable 1m4f handicap for three-year-olds and upwards dates back to 1914 and was formerly known as the Bessborough Handicap (starting out as a sprint) before being renamed in 1999.

## Last year's winner
Candleford, third favourite at 11-2, was a rare seasonal debutant to win (although the second in six years). He was a good fit on draw and age (becoming the 13th successful four-year-old in the last 18 runnings), albeit a touch below the usual ratings band.

## Form
An official rating in the mid-to-high 90s is typical of most runners, and therefore winners, nowadays. To achieve that, most will have been running in Class 2 or 3 handicaps at the better tracks. Six of the last nine

## Key trends
▶ Drawn in double figures, 10/10
▶ Achieved best RPR in a Class 2 or 3 handicap, 10/10
▶ Aged four or five, 9/10 (seven aged four)
▶ Top-three finish last time, 8/10 (six won)
▶ Officially rated between 95 and 99, 7/10

## Other factors
▶ Five of the last ten winners started favourite, including one joint-favourite

winners had won last time out.

## Draw
Candleford last year came from the second-highest stall in a field of 18, making it 14 consecutive winners drawn in double figures. Five of last year's first six came from stall ten or higher, while the unplaced joint-favourites were in three and seven.

## Key races
The 1m4f handicaps at Newmarket's Guineas meeting, York's Dante fixture and the Epsom Derby meeting often provide good guides. Since the last Irish-trained winner (Katiykha in 2000), 14 of the 22 winners had form at one of those meetings and 12 of those had achieved a top-six placing (though only five won).

## Trainers
Sir Michael Stoute has a long and successful history in the race, with six winners, while Mark Johnston (whose yard has now passed to son Charlie) and Hughie Morrison have been two other trainers to note. Remarkably, those three have had 14 of the last 25 winners between them.

## Betting
There have been six successful favourites (outright or joint) in the last 12 runnings after a long gap back to Blueprint in 1999.

### Story of the last ten years

| FORM | WINNER | AGE & WGT | OR | SP | TRAINER | BEST RPR LAST 12 MONTHS (RUNS SINCE) |
|---|---|---|---|---|---|---|
| 22 2d331- | Candleford D | 4 8-12 | 91-5 | 11-2 | William Haggas | won Kempton Class 2 hcap (1m4f) (0) |
| 21 6/13-1 | Quickthorn D | 4 9-3 | 97-6 | 7-2f | Hughie Morrison | won Haydock Class 3 hcap (1m4f) (0) |
| 20 034-5 | Scarlet Dragon D | 7 9-2 | 97-2 | 33-1 | Alan King | 4th Goodwood Class 2 hcap (1m6f) (4) |
| 19 11-31 | Baghdad CD | 4 9-8 | 104-1 | 7-2f | Mark Johnston | won Newmarket Class 2 hcap(1m4f)(0) |
| 18 1-221 | Dash Of Spice D | 4 9-3 | 98T | 7-2f | David Elsworth | won Epsom Class 2 hcap (1m4f) (0) |
| 17 171/8- | Rare Rhythm D | 5 9-2 | 97-4 | 20-1 | Charlie Appleby | Seasonal debut (0) |
| 16 22-01 | Kinema | 5 9-4 | 99-3 | 8-1 | Ralph Beckett | won Goodwood Class 2 hcap (1m6f) (0) |
| 15 342-3 | Arab Dawn BF | 4 9-2 | 96T | 6-1j | Hughie Morrison | 3rd Newmarket Class 2 hcap (1m4f) (0) |
| 14 2-111 | Arab Spring D | 4 9-10 | 104-3 | 11-4f | Sir Michael Stoute | won York Class 2 hcap (1m4f) (0) |
| 13 010-3 | Opinion | 4 9-0 | 95T | 8-1 | Sir Michael Stoute | 3rd Newmarket Class 2 hcap (1m4f) (0) |

**WINS-PL-RUNS** 4yo 7-13-85, 5yo 2-10-47, 6yo+ 1-5-39 **FAVOURITES** £10.75

**FATE OF FAVOURITES** 2112011318 **POSITION OF WINNER IN MARKET** 5114811013

# Shod or unshod

## If you're looking to reduce costs don't compromise on the essentials

*Always consult with your Registered Farrier for both trimming and shoeing needs to ensure the welfare and health of your horse or pony*

Registered Farriers are skilled and qualified professionals who have undergone extensive training and are subject to a Code of Conduct. For further information or to find a Registered Farrier in Great Britain visit **www.farrier-reg.gov.uk**

**frc@farrier-reg.gov.uk**
**01733 319911**
**Farriers Registration Council**

# DAY FOUR

FOUNDED to commemorate the crowning of Queen Victoria in 1838 and first run in 1840, this is the premier race for three-year-old fillies at Royal Ascot and, like the St James's Palace Stakes for colts on day one, often features a clash between the major Guineas winners.

## Last year's winner
Inspiral was unusual in that she was making her seasonal debut, having been forced to miss her intended mission in the 1,000 Guineas following a setback, but she had top-class juvenile form and easily justified favouritism with a near five-length victory for John and Thady Gosden.

**Form** A high level of form at two and/or in the spring Classics is paramount. With any runner who hasn't won a Guineas, the next best indicator is a Group 1 placing at two – 19 of the 23 winners since 2000 fell into one of those two categories. Thirteen of the 23 were either a Guineas winner or a Group 1 winner at two, though only 2013 winner Sky Lantern was both.

**Key races** It is a regular occurrence for the Guineas participants from Britain, Ireland and France to go head to head here. All but three of the 23 winners since 2000 had run in a Guineas,

with eight having been successful in at least one of those Classics and four more placed.

**Trainers** Sir Michael Stoute, who landed his first Coronation with the brilliant Sonic Lady in 1986, has won four times, while Aidan O'Brien and the Gosden stable have been successful on three occasions. This race is an international draw and nine of the last 15 winners were trained outside Britain (five in Ireland, four in France). This is not the only

time in the race's history when overseas raiders have been to the fore. During the period 1989-1996 the race was won by French stables on three occasions (Andre Fabre, Criquette Head and Elie Lellouche) and two Irish yards (Michael Kauntze and John Oxx).

**Betting** Since 2000, Fallen For You (2012) and Watch Me (2019) are the only winners who weren't in the first four in the betting and the only ones sent off bigger than 8-1.

## Key trends

▶ *Adjusted RPR of at least 121, 10/10*
▶ *Rated within 7lb of RPR top-rated, 9/10*
▶ *Ran in a European 1,000 Guineas, 8/10*
▶ *Won earlier in the season, 7/10*

## Other factors

▶ *Four winners had run in the 1,000 Guineas, where they finished 17 15; three ran in France (136) and two in Ireland (11)*
▶ *Winners of the Irish 1,000 Guineas finished 361128*

## Roll of honour

**Longest-priced winner**
25-1 Rebecca Sharp (1997)

**Shortest-priced winner**
1-6 Humble Duty (1970)

*All figures since 1946

**Most successful trainer**
5 wins: **Sir Henry Cecil**
Roussalka (1975), One In A Million (1979), Chalon (1982), Chimes Of Freedom (1990), Kissing Cousin (1994)

**Most successful jockeys**
4 wins: **Joe Mercer**
Festoon (1954), Rosalba (1959), Haymaking (1966), One In A Million (1979)

**Lester Piggott**
Aiming High (1961), Lisadell (1974), Roussalka (1975), Chalon (1982)

**Walter Swinburn**
Sonic Lady (1986), Milligram (1987), Marling (1992), Exclusive (1998)

**Most successful owners**
4 wins: **Niarchos family**
Magic Of Life (1988), Chimes Of Freedom (1990), Alpha Centauri (2018), Alpine Star (2020)

**Cheveley Park Stud**
Exclusive (1998), Russian Rhythm (2003), Nannina (2006), Inspiral (2022)

Frankie Dettori celebrates after riding Inspiral to victory in the Coronation Stakes 12 months ago

## Story of the last ten years

| | FORM | WINNER | AGE | & WGT | Adj RPR | SP | TRAINER | BEST RPR LAST 12 MONTHS (RUNS SINCE) |
|---|---|---|---|---|---|---|---|---|
| 22 | 1111- | **Inspiral** D | 3 | 9-2 | 128ᵀ | 15-8f | John & Thady Gosden | won Fillies' Mile Gp1 (1m) (0) |
| 21 | 21-15 | **Alcohol Free** BF | 3 | 9-0 | 127⁻¹ | 11-2 | Andrew Balding | won Cheveley Park Gp1 (6f) (2) |
| 20 | 311- | **Alpine Star** | 3 | 9-0 | 122⁻⁷ | 9-2 | Jessica Harrington (IRE) | won Debutante Gp2 (7f) (0) |
| 19 | 31-16 | **Watch Me** D | 3 | 9-0 | 121⁻¹⁰ | 20-1 | Francis Graffard (FR) | won Prix Imprudence Gp3 (7f) (1) |
| 18 | 25-01 | **Alpha Centauri** D | 3 | 9-0 | 128⁻¹ | 11-4f | Jessica Harrington (IRE) | won Irish 1,000 Guineas Gp1 (1m) (0 |
| 17 | 1-211 | **Winter** D | 3 | 9-0 | 133ᵀ | 4-9f | Aidan O'Brien (IRE) | won Irish 1,000 Guineas Gp1 (1m) (0) |
| 16 | 13-13 | **Qemah** D, BF | 3 | 9-0 | 127⁻⁴ | 6-1 | Jean-Claude Rouget (FR) | won Prix de la Grotte Gp3 (1m) (1) |
| 15 | 32-11 | **Ervedya** D | 3 | 9-0 | 129⁻¹ | 3-1 | Jean-Claude Rouget (FR) | won Prix Imprudence Gp3 (7f) (1) |
| 14 | 312-7 | **Rizeena** C | 3 | 9-0 | 127ᵀ | 11-2 | Clive Brittain | won Moyglare Stud Stakes Gp1 (7f) (2) |
| 13 | 18-21 | **Sky Lantern** D | 3 | 9-0 | 127ᵀ | 9-2j | Richard Hannon snr | won 1,000 Guineas Gp1 (1m) (0) |

**FAVOURITES** £0.82

**TRAINERS IN THIS RACE** (w-pl-r) Jessica Harrington 2-1-3, Jean-Claude Rouget 2-1-3, Aidan O'Brien 1-5-16, Andrew Balding 1-0-3, Francis Graffard 1-0-1, John & Thady Gosden 1-0-2, Richard Hannon 0-1-5, Ralph Beckett 0-0-2

**FATE OF FAVOURITES** 1026112351 **POSITION OF WINNER IN MARKET** 1324117331

# DAY FOUR 5.00 Sandringham Stakes

NTRODUCED to the Royal Ascot programme in 2002, this is a handicap for three-year-old fillies rated 0-105 run over the straight mile, making it effectively a fillies' version of the Britannia.

## Last year's winner

Heredia was higher in the weights than a typical winner and raced down the centre (which was the place to be on this occasion), scoring by a length for Richard Hannon as 7-2 favourite and then surviving a stewards' inquiry into late interference.

**Form** Thirteen of the 21 winners had already tasted success that season (nine were last-time-out winners) and Heredia joined Muteela (2014) and Persuasive (2016) in going to Royal Ascot unbeaten in three previous starts.

**Draw** Racing on one of the two wings tends to be an

advantage. The trends point to a draw in the six highest or five lowest stalls.

**Key races** A good test is important in preparation for this fast-paced race, either in Group/Listed company or a decent-sized field in a handicap. Eleven of the 21 winners had already won over a mile or further.

**Trainers** Hannon last year became the fourth trainer to notch two wins, having also scored with Osaila in 2015. The other notable one recently is Charlie Fellowes,

who had back-to-back wins with Thanks Be (2019) and Onassis (2020).

**Betting** Despite the race's large number of runners and hugely competitive nature, it is notable that fancied contenders do well. Eleven of the 21 winners came from the top two in the betting, including seven who had at least a share of favouritism, and only five winners have been bigger than 11-1 (although two of the last four were 33-1, both trained by Fellowes).

## Key trends
- Lost maiden tag, 9/10
- Drawn in the six highest or the five lowest stalls, 8/10
- Carried no more than 9st 2lb, 7/10
- Won over 7f or a mile earlier that season, 7/10
- No more than three juvenile starts, 6/10

## Other factors
- Six winners ran in handicaps as three-year-olds (five won at least one; exception finished second)
- Three winners had contested a Listed or Group race at three

### Story of the last ten years

| FORM | WINNER | AGE & WGT | OR | SP | TRAINER | BEST RPR LAST 12 MONTHS (RUNS SINCE) |
|---|---|---|---|---|---|---|
| 22 11-1 | **Heredia** | 3 9-8 | 98T | 7-2f | Richard Hannon | won York Class 3 hcap (7f) (0) |
| 21 3-101 | **Create Belief** D | 3 9-2 | 97T | 6-1 | Johnny Murtagh (IRE) | won Curragh hcap (1m) (0) |
| 20 7251- | **Onassis** | 3 8-1 | 81-14 | 33-1 | Charlie Fellowes | won Newcastle Class 4 hcap (7f) (0) |
| 19 55-22 | **Thanks Be** (4oh) | 3 8-0 | 84-6 | 33-1 | Charlie Fellowes | 2nd Nottingham Class 4 hcp (1m2f) (0) |
| 18 6-21 | **Agrotera** D | 3 8-7 | 88-5 | 11-2f | Ed Walker | 2nd Ascot Class 3 cond (1m) (1) |
| 17 142-4 | **Con Te Partiro** | 3 9-5 | 102-12 | 20-1 | Wesley Ward (USA) | 4th Belmont Park Listed (7f) (0) |
| 16 1-11 | **Persuasive** | 3 8-9 | 95T | 11-4f | John Gosden | won Chelmsford Class 2 hcp (1m) (0) |
| 15 13-17 | **Osaila** CD | 3 9-7 | 107-3 | 13-2 | Richard Hannon | 5th Moyglare Stud Stakes Gp1 (7f) (4) |
| 14 1-11 | **Muteela** | 3 8-13 | 95T | 9-2f | Mark Johnston | won Newmarket Class 3 hcap (1m) (0) |
| 13 41-61 | **Annecdote** (1oh) | 3 8-7 | 91T | 11-1 | Jonathan Portman | won Newbury Class 4 hcap (7f) (0) |

**FAVOURITES** £10.25

**FATE OF FAVOURITES** 0121010P21 **POSITION OF WINNER IN MARKET** 5121910921

Irish Injured Jockeys was set up in 2014 to increase awareness and raise vital funds to support our injured jockeys. Funds raised through Irish Injured Jockeys go to the injured riders who are most in need of support. Our aim is to make a difference to the lives and welfare of jockeys past and present, and their families by using funds donated by the public

www.irishinjuredjockeys.com

DATING back to 1834, this Group 2 over 1m4f for three-year-olds comes just under three weeks after the Derby at Epsom and was once officially called the Ascot Derby, as it still is colloquially, such is the close link between the races.

**Last year's winner** In a field of six, Aidan O'Brien's Changingoftheguard was well clear on Racing Post Ratings and justified 11-10 favouritism, albeit by just a short head from 10-1 shot Grand Alliance, who was the other runner to head here after the Derby.

**Form** Changingoftheguard was typical of most winners in not having been highly tried at two (three maiden runs without success) before improving at three to contest a Derby trial (and the big

### Key trends
▶ *Won within last three starts, 10/10*
▶ *Adjusted RPR of at least 118, 9/10*
▶ *Yet to win over 1m4f, 8/10*
▶ *Within 5lb of RPR top-rated, 8/10 (the last eight)*
▶ *Ran in a recognised Derby trial, 8/10 (four won)*
▶ *Top-three finish last time out, 6/10*

### Other factors
▶ *The only two winners who had run in Group company as juveniles were Japan and Pyledriver (Japan won a Group 2)*

race itself). He had an RPR of 89 at two but was up to 114 by the time he arrived at Royal Ascot.

**Key races** Even though there is only a short time between Epsom and Royal Ascot, many King Edward VII winners have graduated from the Derby, including four of the last six under the normal schedule (not including the lockdown year of 2020 when the races were the other way round). Across The Stars (2016) and Permian (2018) both finished tenth on the Downs, while Japan (2019) was third and Changingoftheguard fifth last year.

**Trainers** Sir Michael Stoute has won the race seven times. The stables built up by Mark Johnston and John Gosden have had three winners apiece. O'Brien (also on three in total) has had two winners and five runners-up in the past decade.

**Betting** Twenty of the last 25 winners have been no bigger than 7-1.

## Story of the last ten years

| | FORM | WINNER | | AGE & WGT | Adj RPR | SP | TRAINER | BEST RPR LAST 12 MONTHS (RUNS SINCE) |
|---|---|---|---|---|---|---|---|---|
| 22 | 2-115 | **Changingoftheguard** | D | 3 9-2 | 126$^T$ | 11-10f | Aidan O'Brien (IRE) | won Chester Vase Gp3 (1m4½f) (1) |
| 21 | 12-1 | **Alenquer** | | 3 9-0 | 123$^T$ | 13-8f | William Haggas | won Sandown Classic Trial Gp3 (1m2f) (0) |
| 20 | 417-2 | **Pyledriver** | | 3 9-0 | 118$^{-5}$ | 18-1 | William Muir | 2nd Classic Trial Gp3 (1m2f) (0) |
| 19 | 11-43 | **Japan** | | 3 9-0 | 132$^T$ | 6-4f | Aidan O'Brien (IRE) | 3rd Derby Gp1 (1m4f) (0) |
| 18 | 7-121 | **Old Persian** | | 3 9-0 | 120$^{-4}$ | 9-2 | Charlie Appleby | won Newmarket Listed (1m2f) (0) |
| 17 | 32110 | **Permian** | | 3 9-0 | 128$^T$ | 6-1 | Mark Johnston | won Dante Stakes Gp2 (1m2½f) (1) |
| 16 | 2-130 | **Across The Stars** | D | 3 9-0 | 120$^{-2}$ | 7-1 | Sir Michael Stoute | 3rd Lingfield Derby Trial Listed (1m3½f) (1) |
| 15 | 1-2 | **Balios** | | 3 9-0 | 123$^{-5}$ | 3-1 | David Simcock | 2nd Newmarket Stakes Listed (1m2f) (0) |
| 14 | 14 | **Eagle Top** BF | | 3 9-0 | 114$^{-10}$ | 12-1 | John Gosden | 4th Leicester Class 3 hcap (1m4f) (0) |
| 13 | 41-22 | **Hillstar** BF | | 3 8-12 | 118$^{-13}$ | 15-2 | Sir Michael Stoute | 2nd Newbury Class 2 hcap (1m2f) (0) |

**FAVOURITES** -£2.78

**TRAINERS IN THIS RACE** (w-pl-r) Sir Michael Stoute 2-1-6, Aidan O'Brien 2-6-16, William Haggas 1-0-5, Charlie Appleby 1-0-4, Michael Bell 0-1-1, Andrew Balding 0-2-4, Roger Varian 0-2-3, Ralph Beckett 0-0-3

**FATE OF FAVOURITES** 22P2351411 **POSITION OF WINNER IN MARKET** 3624231511

# 6.10 Palace of Holyroodhouse Stakes

NTRODUCED as part of Royal Ascot's expanded programme in 2020, this five-furlong handicap for three-year-olds rated 0-105 has tended towards high-numbered stalls in the first three runnings.

In 2020 6-4 favourite Art Power came out of stall 19 to win easily from Keep Busy (drawn 21); in 2021 the first four all came from the five highest berths (Significantly won from stall 24 at 10-1); and last year five of the first six were from 21 or higher, although 5-1 winner Latin Lover came out of stall 11.

The first two winners carried 9st 1lb and 9st, although Art Power had an official rating of 97 while Significantly was on 90, and last year Latin Lover got in near the bottom on 8st 2lb (rated 84). No horse from the top six in the weights has made the first four in the three runnings.

Celebrations after Latin Lover's victory 12 months ago under Hayley Turner

# EXPERT VIEW

Racing Post big-race trends expert Kevin Morley picks out a
key pointer for each of the five days. Read all his key trends in
our race-by-race guide

# Key trends

## TUESDAY

The Palace House Stakes run at Newmarket's Guineas meeting is Britain's best trial for the King's Stand and, while that wouldn't appear to be a great revelation, it's a factor that seems to be underestimated by the market. Over the last 20 years, 13 Palace House winners have lined up and five have followed up at the royal meeting, returning SPs of 9-2, 8-1, 5-1, 20-1 and 4-1 (38 per cent strike-rate, +33.50pts level-stake profit). The winner of the Newmarket Group 3 sprint (soft-ground lover Vadream this year) is also worth bearing in mind for each-way purposes as only three of those 13 finished outside the first four.

## THURSDAY

Five of the last ten winners of the Hampton Court Stakes had run in a handicap. There have been 105 runners in the race across the last decade with 21 of those coming through the handicap ranks. However, just looking at those who came into Ascot on the back of a win narrows that down to nine and still finds all five winners at prices of 9-4, 7-4, 15-8, 11-2 and 11-8 (56 per cent, +8.75pts to level stakes).

## FRIDAY

A high draw is usually best in the Albany and the race certainly favours fillies with plenty of scope for improvement. Looking at those drawn 13 or higher with two runs or fewer under their belt finds eight of the last ten winners from 59 qualifiers (14 per cent, +28.50pts)

## SATURDAY

It usually pays to side with an in-form four-year-old in the Hardwicke. There have been 26 runners from that age group who achieved a top-two finish on their most recent outing, with seven obliging and returning a healthy +26.82pts level-stake profit (27 per cent).

## WEDNESDAY

Four-year-olds tend to fare best in the Royal Hunt Cup and focusing on those rated 94-103, carrying no more than 9st 3lb with an SP 25-1 or less finds six winners from 55 qualifiers (11 per cent). With the winners returned at 8-1, 25-1, 16-1, 15-2, 18-1 and 13-2, including the last three, the system provides a 32pts level-stake profit.

# DAY FIVE

A sizzling Saturday lies in store with top sprinters, early juveniles, up-and-coming three-year-olds, classy older horses, battle-hardened handicappers and out-and-out stayers on the bill.

Last year's final day was typically action-packed, with tight finishes, big-priced shocks and a couple of popular returning winners.

The Group 1 highlight is the Queen Elizabeth II Jubilee Stakes, renamed in memory of the late monarch. This six-furlong sprint for older horses has a reputation for attracting the best sprinters from all parts of the globe, with winners from Australia, Hong Kong and the United States in recent years. Godolphin had the one-two last year, led by 33-1 shot Naval Crown.

Immediately before the big sprint is the Group 2 Hardwicke Stakes, a long-established Royal Ascot favourite and regularly a pointer to the King George VI and Queen Elizabeth Stakes at the royal track in July.

The other Group race on the card is the Jersey Stakes, a Group 3 over seven furlongs that is often a proving ground for a star three-year-old in the making.

The two-year-olds open the card in the seven-furlong Chesham Stakes, which attracts those who are likely to excel at a mile or further during their three-year-old careers.

Churchill, who went on to land the 2,000 Guineas and Irish 2,000 Guineas in 2017, scored his first career success in this race, while 2018 Derby winner Masar was third in his attempt. Last year Holloway Boy took the prize at 40-1, becoming the first debutant to win at Royal Ascot since 1996.

The last heritage handicap of the week is the Wokingham Stakes over six furlongs, which attracts a big field of up to 30 runners and a competitive betting market. Rohaan, carrying top weight, made it back-to-back wins last year at 18-1.

That is followed by the Golden Gates Stakes, a 1m2f handicap for three-year-olds that joined the bill in 2020, and the royal meeting closes with the Queen Alexandra Stakes, won for the past two years by the Willie Mullins-trained Stratum.

The long-established test over nearly two and three-quarter miles is a much-loved traditional ending to a meeting steeped in history.

# Saturday June 24

2.30 **Chesham Stakes** (Listed)      **7f** 2yo      £100,000
Last year's winner: Holloway Boy 40-1

3.05 **Jersey Stakes** (Group 3)      **7f** 3yo      £150,000
Last year's winner: Noble Truth 4-1f

3.40 **Hardwicke Stakes** (Group 2)      **1m4f** 4yo+      £250,000
Last year's winner: Broome 6-1

4.20 **Queen Elizabeth II Jubilee Stakes** (Group 1)      **6f** 4yo+      £1,000,000
Last year's winner: Naval Crown 33-1

5.00 **Wokingham Stakes** (Heritage Handicap)      **6f** 3yo+      £175,000
Last year's winner: Rohaan 18-1

5.35 **Golden Gates Stakes** (Handicap)      **1m2f** 3yo      £100,000
Last year's winner: Missed The Cut 5-2f

6.10 **Queen Alexandra Stakes** (Conditions)      **2m6f** 4yo+      £100,000
Last year's winner: Stratum 10-1

Race value is total prize-money

ROYAL ASCOT

FIRST run in 1919, this Listed contest is the final race of the meeting for two-year-olds and at seven furlongs is the longest of the week for that age group. It is open only to horses whose sire or dam won over a distance in excess of nine and a half furlongs.

**Last year's winner**

Holloway Boy broke most of the trends, winning at 40-1 on his debut (with the placed horses 80-1 and 33-1). He was the first newcomer to win at Royal Ascot since 1996 (when Shamikh did it in this race and Dazzle in the Windsor Castle Stakes).

**Form** Since the race distance was raised to seven furlongs in 1996, most of the 27 winners had raced only once, with 18 having won (14 had won their sole start).

**Key trends**
▶ *Rated within 11lb of RPR top-rated, eight winners in last ten runnings*
▶ *Raced just once, 8/10 (four had won)*
▶ *By a sire with a stamina index of at least 8.7f, 7/10*
▶ *Recorded Topspeed figure of at least 63, 6/10*
▶ *Adjusted RPR of at least 91, 6/10*

**Other factors**
▶ *Since Bach in 1999, only two winners had previously scored over 7f – September in 2017 and Point Lonsdale in 2021 (all trained by Aidan O'Brien)*
▶ *The record of fillies is 1-27*

**Key races** Before Holloway Boy (who hadn't run), six of the other nine winners in the past decade had made their debut less than four weeks

before this race. Only two had run over 7f. Curragh, Newbury and Newmarket maidens are often an indicator of high regard.

**Trainers** It is no surprise that Aidan O'Brien – the dominant force in Classics both at a mile and over middle distances – has won four times in the last seven years. Interestingly, those four winners came in years when he fielded just a single representative. Also keep a close eye on John and Thady Gosden and Godolphin trainers Charlie Appleby and Saeed bin Suroor. Between them, those named trainers have won eight of the last 12 runnings.

**Betting** Since 1996, nine of the 27 winners had market leadership, with a further 13 in the top four in the betting.

## Story of the last ten years

| FORM | | WINNER | AGE & WGT | Adj RPR | SP | TRAINER | BEST RPR LAST 12 MONTHS (RUNS SINCE) |
|------|----|--------|-----------|---------|------|---------|--------------------------------------|
| 22 | | **Holloway Boy** | 2 9-5 | | 40-1 | Karl Burke | Debutant |
| 21 | 1 | **Point Lonsdale** D | 2 9-3 | 106$^T$ | 10-11f | Aidan O'Brien (IRE) | won Curragh maiden (7f) (0) |
| 20 | 5 | **Battleground** | 2 9-3 | 90$^6$ | 11-4f | Aidan O'Brien (IRE) | 5th Naas maiden (6f) (0) |
| 19 | 11 | **Pinatubo** | 2 9-3 | 107$^T$ | 3-1 | Charlie Appleby | won Epsom Class 2 cond (6f) (0) |
| 18 | 1 | **Arthur Kitt** | 2 9-3 | 100$^9$ | 13-2 | Tom Dascombe | won Haydock Class 4 novice (6f) (0) |
| 17 | 1 | **September** D | 2 8-12 | 107$^T$ | 11-8f | Aidan O'Brien (IRE) | won Leopardstown maiden (7f) (0) |
| 16 | 3 | **Churchill** BF | 2 9-3 | 95$^9$ | 8-11f | Aidan O'Brien (IRE) | 3rd Curragh maiden (6f) (0) |
| 15 | 1 | **Sunny Way** | 2 9-3 | 91$^7$ | 14-1 | Eoghan O'Neill (FR) | won Maisons-Laffitte maiden (6f) (0) |
| 14 | 4 | **Richard Pankhurst** BF | 2 9-3 | 87$^{23}$ | 10-1 | John Gosden | 4th Newmarket Class 4 maiden (6f) (0) |
| 13 | 3 | **Berkshire** | 2 9-3 | 90$^{11}$ | 16-1 | Paul Cole | 3rd Newbury Class 4 maiden (6f) (0) |

**FAVOURITES** £-0.24

**TRAINERS IN THIS RACE** (w-pl-r) Aidan O'Brien 4-3-13, Charlie Appleby 1-1-6, Karl Burke 1-0-2, Saeed bin Suroor 0-1-2, Richard Hannon 0-0-7, Andrew Balding 0-1-5, John & Thady Gosden 0-1-4, Paul & Oliver Cole 0-0-1

**FATE OF FAVOURITES** 2321102116 **POSITION OF WINNER IN MARKET** 8461132110

DATING back to 1919, this Group 3 race for three-year-olds over seven furlongs is a battleground between Classic pretenders dropping back from a mile and sprinters trying to stretch out their stamina.

**Last year's winner** Noble Truth, coming off a career-best Listed win at Newmarket in April, had all the right credentials apart from going through a Classic campaign. He justified favouritism by a length from 40-1 outsider Find My Love.

**Form** Most winners had been highly tried already and that is evident when looking at their two-year-old records. Eighteen of the last 20 winners raced at two but perhaps more telling is the fact that, among them, 14

## Key trends
▶ *Adjusted RPR of at least 122, 8/10*
▶ *First or second in one or both of last two starts, 8/10*
▶ *Rated within 5lb of RPR top-rated, 8/10*
▶ *Ran in a Classic trial, 6/10*

## Other factors
▶ *Five winners had yet to win as a three-year-old.*
▶ *Five winners had run in a Guineas.*

had a first-four finish at Group level during their juvenile season. That high level is further illustrated by the peak RPRs of winners heading into the race, with 17 of the last 20 winners having run to 106-plus.

**Key races** Until recently the trend was for those who had run in a Guineas to hold

sway, with eight out of ten winners up to 2018 having done so, but none of the last four winners came down that route. Space Traveller in 2019 and Creative Force in 2021 had both run in the Listed Carnarvon Stakes at Newbury, finishing third and first, and last year Noble Truth had won the Listed King Charles II Stakes at Newmarket.

**Trainers** Sir Michael Stoute holds the record with six wins, stretching back to his Royal Ascot breakthrough with Etienne Gerard in 1977. Godolphin trainers have won three of the last seven runnings.

**Betting** Noble Truth last year became the fifth successful favourite in the past decade (two other winners were in the top three in the betting).

### Story of the last ten years

| | FORM | WINNER | AGE & WGT | Adj RPR | SP | TRAINER | BEST RPR LAST 12 MONTHS (RUNS SINCE) |
|---|---|---|---|---|---|---|---|
| 22 | 24-01 | **Noble Truth** D | 3 9-3 | 125-1 | 4-1f | Charlie Appleby | won Newmarket Listed (7f) (0) |
| 21 | 0-111 | **Creative Force** | 3 9-1 | 128T | 5-1j | Charlie Appleby | won Newbury Listed (6f) (0) |
| 20 | 2114- | **Molatham** D, BF | 3 9-1 | 123-2 | 11-2 | Roger Varian | won Doncaster Listed (7f) (1) |
| 19 | 7-237 | **Space Traveller** | 3 9-1 | 116-10 | 25-1 | Richard Fahey | 2nd Maisons-Laffitte Gp3 (6f) (5) |
| 18 | 19-20 | **Expert Eye** D | 3 9-1 | 129T | 8-1 | Sir Michael Stoute | won Vintage Stakes Gp2 (7f) (3) |
| 17 | 1-12 | **Le Brivido** | 3 9-1 | 131T | 2-1f | Andre Fabre (FR) | 2nd Poule d'Essai des Poulains Gp1 (1m) (0) |
| 16 | 1-2d3 | **Ribchester** | 3 9-6 | 122-5 | 7-1 | Richard Fahey | won Mill Reef Stakes Gp2 (6f) (2) |
| 15 | 113-7 | **Dutch Connection** D | 3 9-4 | 118-9 | 14-1 | Charlie Hills | 3rd National Stakes Gp1 (7f) (1) |
| 14 | 12-13 | **Mustajeeb** D | 3 9-4 | 124-4 | 9-2j | Dermot Weld (IRE) | won Amethyst Stakes Gp3 (1m) (1) |
| 13 | 3-142 | **Gale Force Ten** D | 3 9-1 | 128T | 9-2f | Aidan O'Brien (IRE) | 2nd Irish 2,000 Guineas Gp1 (1m) (0) |

**FAVOURITES** £9.25

**TRAINERS IN THIS RACE** (w-pl-r) Charlie Appleby 2-2-6, Richard Fahey 2-0-6, Aidan O'Brien 1-4-16, Roger Varian 1-1-8, Charlie Hills 1-0-9, Sir Michael Stoute 1-2-4, Andre Fabre 1-0-1, Andrew Balding 0-1-6, William Haggas 0-2-7, Saeed bin Suroor 0-1-8, John & Thady Gosden 0-1-4

**FATE OF FAVOURITES** 1106102611 **POSITION OF WINNER IN MARKET** 1162130411

# 3.40 Hardwicke Stakes

First run in 1879, this Group 2 race over 1m4f is for four-year-olds and upwards and often provides a showcase for horses who were in the Derby picture the previous year.

## Last year's winner

Six-year-old globetrotter Broome became the oldest winner since 2007, having been runner-up in this race 12 months earlier. As a multiple Group winner, including at the top level, he was well up to the usual class in this contest and scored decisively by three and a quarter lengths.

## Form

An adjusted RPR of 128 has been the minimum standard required since 2010 and most winners have been in the 130s, which points to a Group 1 performer. Four of the last ten winners had

### Key trends

▶ Group-race winner, 10/10
▶ Adjusted RPR of at least 128, 10/10
▶ Rated within 8lb of RPR top-rated, 10/10
▶ Distance winner, 9/10
▶ Aged four, 8/10
▶ Top-two finish last time out, 8/10
▶ Finished in the first three in a Listed or Group race that season, 7/10

### Other factors

▶ Five winners scored last time out
▶ Three winners were RPR top-rated

run in a Group 1 last time and three of the others were coming off victory in a lower-level Group race.

## Key races

All but two of the last 15 winners were aged four and many had followed

similar career paths to this point, with nine of them having competed the previous year in at least one of the St Leger, the Great Voltigeur Stakes at York or the King Edward VII Stakes at Royal Ascot.

## Trainers

This is Sir Michael Stoute's best race at Royal Ascot with 11 winners, eight of them in the last 17 runnings, and Aidan O'Brien has had four winners, all since 2008. Mark Johnston (whose licence has passed to son Charlie) had four winners, although the most recent was Bandari in 2005.

## Betting

The market has been a good guide recently, with 13 of the last 17 winners coming from the first three in the betting. Six of the seven successful favourites in that period were trained by Stoute or O'Brien.

## Story of the last ten years

| | FORM | WINNER | | AGE & WGT | Adj RPR | SP | TRAINER | BEST RPR LAST 12 MONTHS (RUNS SINCE) |
|---|---|---|---|---|---|---|---|---|
| 22 | 020-5 | Broome | D | 6 9-3 | 132-4 | 6-1 | Aidan O'Brien (IRE) | 2nd Breeders' Cup Turf Gp1 (1m4f) (1) |
| 21 | 1511- | Wonderful Tonight | CD | 4 8-12 | 135-1 | 5-1 | David Menuisier | won Fillies & Mares Gp1 (1m4f) (0) |
| 20 | 114-2 | Fanny Logan | BF | 4 8-12 | 128-7 | 17-2 | John Gosden | 2nd Haydock Gp3 (1m3½f) (0) |
| 19 | 2-421 | Defoe | D | 5 9-1 | 135T | 11-4f | Roger Varian | won Coronation Cup Gp1 (1m4f) (0) |
| 18 | 12-11 | Crystal Ocean | D | 4 9-1 | 135T | 4-7f | Sir Michael Stoute | won Aston Park Stakes Gp3 (1m4f) (0) |
| 17 | 1U5-6 | Idaho | D | 4 9-1 | 133-1 | 9-2 | Aidan O'Brien (IRE) | 2nd Irish Derby Gp1 (1m4f) (4) |
| 16 | 53-11 | Dartmouth | CD | 4 9-1 | 129-7 | 10-1 | Sir Michael Stoute | won Ormonde Stakes Gp3 (1m5½f) (0) |
| 15 | 237-1 | Snow Sky | D | 4 9-1 | 130-8 | 12-1 | Sir Michael Stoute | won Yorkshire Cup Gp2 (1m6f) (0) |
| 14 | 21-22 | Telescope | D | 4 9-1 | 130T | 7-4f | Sir Michael Stoute | 2nd Huxley Stakes Gp3 (1m2½f) (0) |
| 13 | 58-22 | Thomas Chippendale | CD | 4 9-0 | 129-6 | 8-1 | Lady Cecil | won King Edward VII Stakes Gp2 (1m4f) (4) |

**WINS-RUNS** 4yo 8-8-42, 5yo 1-7-23, 6yo+ 1-2-20 **FAVOURITES** -£1.93

**TRAINERS IN THIS RACE** (w-pl-r) Sir Michael Stoute 4-2-14, Aidan O'Brien 2-2-10, Roger Varian 1-2-7, David Menuisier 1-0-1, John & Thady Gosden 0-1-1, Owen Burrows 0-1-1, Andrew Balding 0-1-3, Charlie Appleby 0-0-2, William Haggas 0-0-3

**FATE OF FAVOURITES** S160411523 **POSITION OF WINNER IN MARKET** 4146211633

# SO MUCH MORE THAN A MUSEUM!

NHRM occupies a 5-acre site in the heart of Newmarket and provides a wonderful day out for all ages.

Using the latest interactive and audio-visual displays you can find out about the history of horseracing, enjoy some of the country's best examples of sporting art, meet former racehorses, have a go on the racehorse simulator and watch the sparks fly as a farrier works in the forge.

EXPLORE GREAT EXHIBITIONS, BROWSE OUR GIFT SHOP & BOOKSTORE.

DISCOVER THE RESTAURANT AND BAKERY AT NHRM

**National Horseracing Museum**  Palace Street, Newmarket, Suffolk, CB8 8EP

@NHRMuseum

Book Online: www.nhrm.co.uk

# DAY FIVE

NAUGURATED in 1868 and long known as the Cork and Orrery Stakes, this has held Group 1 status since 2002 when it was renamed first to celebrate the golden jubilee of Queen Elizabeth II. This is the big 6f sprint of the week for older horses (open only to four-year-olds and upwards since the advent of the Commonwealth Cup for three-year-olds).

**Last year's winner** Naval Crown, who missed a couple of key trends on RPR and recent form, caused a 33-1 upset in a one-two for Charlie Appleby, snatching victory from 12-1 stablemate Creative Force by a neck.

**Form** Most winners bring a strong level of form, with 17 out of 21 since the upgrade to Group 1 having been placed at least in this grade in the previous 12 months (11 had won). The other four had at least competed at that level. Naval Crown had been fourth in the Group 1 Al Quoz Sprint at Meydan last time out.

**Key races** The British Champions Sprint, run over course and distance the previous October, is a key guide. Five of the last eight British or Irish winners had run there, finishing 12188, with the exceptions being 2018 winner Merchant Navy, who was trained by Aidan O'Brien but had

arrived only recently from Australia, and Godolphin's Blue Point and Naval Crown, who had been sent to Dubai for the winter.

The best prep race has been the Duke of York Stakes, with five of the 14 British-trained winners since 2002 having run there for finishing positions of 03255 (O'Brien's Starspangledbanner also prepped there in 2010, finishing fifth).

One explanation for the step up in performance from the Duke of York (and the fact that only seven of the last 21 winners had scored on their previous outing) is that the ground often changes from softish in

May to much faster in June. Fifteen of the last 21 runnings have been contested on good to firm (or firm) and 12 of the 15 winners in those years had already won on that kind of surface.

The main races to check for the type who has been placed in a Group 1 but not yet won at that level are the previous year's running of this race, the July Cup and Haydock Sprint Cup.

**Trainers** Appleby is the only trainer with more than one win in the past ten runnings, having scored with Blue Point (also a dual winner of the King's Stand Stakes) and Naval Crown.

# 4.20 Queen Elizabeth II Jubilee Stakes

Naval Crown (right) wins
last year at 33-1

**Betting** Since the race was upgraded to Group 1 nine of the 21 winners were priced in double figures, with only five successful favourites.

## Roll of honour

**Longest-priced winner**
40-1 Kearney (1980)

**Shortest-priced winner**
1-6 Black Caviar (2012)

**Most successful trainer**
5 wins: **Vincent O'Brien**
Welsh Saint (1970), Saritamer (1974), Swingtime (1975), Thatching (1979), College Chapel (1993)

**Most successful jockey**
9 wins: **Lester Piggott**
Right Boy (1958, 1959), Tin Whistle (1960), El Gallo (1963), Mountain Call (1968), Welsh Saint (1970), Saritamer (1974), Thatching (1979), College Chapel (1993)

**Most successful owner**
3 wins: **Godolphin**
So Factual (1995), Blue Point (2019), Naval Crown (2022)

*All figures since 1946

## Key trends

▸ *Adjusted RPR of at least 127, 9/10*
▸ *No older than five, 9/10*
▸ *Top-three finish within last two starts, 9/10*
▸ *Group or Listed winner over 6f, 8/10*

## Other factors

▸ *Five winners had yet to score earlier in the season.*
▸ *Three winners had run in the race the year before, finishing 782, while seven winners had contested a previous Royal Ascot (one won, three placed and three unplaced).*

## Story of the last ten years

| | FORM | WINNER | AGE & WGT | Adj RPR | SP | TRAINER | BEST RPR LAST 12 MONTHS (RUNS SINCE) |
|---|---|---|---|---|---|---|---|
| 22 | 8-104 | **Naval Crown** | 4 9-5 | 123-11 | 33-1 | Charlie Appleby | 4th Al Quoz Sprint Gp1 (6f) (0) |
| 21 | 118-1 | **Dream Of Dreams** D | 7 9-3 | 134T | 3-1f | Sir Michael Stoute | won Windsor Listed (6f) (0) |
| 20 | 1318- | **Hello Youmzain** D | 4 9-3 | 132T | 4-1 | Kevin Ryan | won Haydock Sprint Cup Gp1(6f) (1) |
| 19 | -1111 | **Blue Point** CD | 5 9-3 | 137T | 6-4f | Charlie Appleby | won King's Stand Gp1 (5f) (0) |
| 18 | 1-331 | **Merchant Navy** D | 4 9-3 | 131-8 | 4-1 | Aidan O'Brien (IRE) | won Curragh Gp2 (6f) (0) |
| 17 | 121-5 | **The Tin Man** CD | 5 9-3 | 132-5 | 9-2 | James Fanshawe | won Champions Sprint Gp1 (6f) (1) |
| 16 | 112-5 | **Twilight Son** D | 4 9-3 | 132T | 7-2 | Henry Candy | 2nd Champions Sprint Gp1 (6f) (1) |
| 15 | 33-32 | **Undrafted** D | 5 9-3 | 127-8 | 14-1 | Wesley Ward (USA) | 3rd Breeders' Cup Turf Sprint Gd1 (6½f) (2) |
| 14 | 210-1 | **Slade Power** CD | 5 9-4 | 131T | 7-2f | Eddie Lynam (IRE) | won Curragh Gp3 (6f) (0) |
| 13 | 130-2 | **Lethal Force** | 4 9-4 | 128-6 | 11-1 | Clive Cox | 2nd Duke of York Stakes Gp2 (6f) (0) |

**WINS-RUNS** 3yo 0-1-4, 4yo 5-10-64, 5yo 4-5-44, 6yo+ 1-5-38 **FAVOURITES** £1.00

**TRAINERS IN THIS RACE** (w-pl-r) Charlie Appleby 2-1-5, Aidan O'Brien 1-1-8, Wesley Ward 1-2-5, Kevin Ryan 1-1-4, Henry Candy 1-1-5, Clive Cox 1-0-4, James Fanshawe 1-1-6, Tim Easterby 0-1-2, William Haggas 0-1-5, Andrew Balding 0-0-6

**FATE OF FAVOURITES** 2124301310 **POSITION OF WINNER IN MARKET** 6163221210

# DAY FIVE                              5.00 Wokingham Stakes

DATING back to 1813, this is the last heritage handicap of the week and one of the big handicap sprints of the Flat season, with up to 30 runners charging down the straight in a hotly contested 6f race.

## Last year's winner

Rohaan became the first back-to-back winner since Selhurstpark Flyer (1997 & 1998), scoring off top weight at 18-1. Apart from his course-and-distance form, he didn't hit many key trends in completing his remarkable feat.

**Form** The class factor has been important, with ten of the last 17 winners no more than 2lb off top-rated on Racing Post Ratings. The importance of getting into the race on the right sort of handicap mark is evident in the fact that only four of

## Key trends
▶ Distance winner, 9/10
▶ Officially rated between 99 and 107, 8/10
▶ Aged four or five, 8/10 (six aged five)
▶ Rated within 6lb of RPR top-rated, 8/10
▶ Top-four finish last time out, 7/10
▶ Won over 7f, 7/10

## Other factors
▶ Four winners were drawn between 12 and 22, four in one to 11 and two between 23 and 31
▶ Five winners had won or placed in a field of at least 18 runners

those 17 winners had won that season, although 11 had achieved a top-four finish last time out.

**Draw** Recent runnings suggest the winner can come from anywhere on the track, although by a strange quirk three of the last four winners have come out of stall ten.

**Weight** Winners have tended to come from a narrow weights range, from 8st 12lb to 9st 3lb, although four of the last five have carried 9st 6lb-plus. Only two of the last ten winners were not in triple figures on

official marks (and both were only just outside on 99).

**Key races** The Victoria Cup at Ascot can be significant, along with the Class 2 6f handicap at York's Dante meeting.

**Trainers** Newmarket stables have the best long-term record but northern trainers have won four of the last ten runnings.

**Betting** Even though only two favourites have won since 2005, nine of the 17 winners since then were in the first four in the market.

### Story of the last ten years

| FORM | WINNER | | AGE & WGT | OR | SP | TRAINER | BEST RPR LAST 12 MONTHS (RUNS SINCE) |
|------|--------|--|-----------|-----|-----|---------|--------------------------------------|
| 22 | 0-878 | **Rohaan** CD | 4 9-12 | 109-9 | 18-1 | David Evans | won Wokingham hcap (6f) (7) |
| 21 | 21511 | **Rohaan** CD | 3 9-8 | 112-10 | 8-1 | David Evans | won Sandy Lane Gp2 (6f) (0) |
| 20 | 000-0 | **Hey Jonesy** D | 5 9-3 | 99-1 | 18-1 | Kevin Ryan | 2nd Haydock Class 3 cond (7f) (4) |
| 19 | 227-1 | **Cape Byron** C | 5 9-9 | 107-4 | 7-2f | Roger Varian | won Victoria Cup hcap (7f) (0) |
| 18 | 5314- | **Bacchus** D | 4 9-6 | 105-6 | 33-1 | Brian Meehan | won Newmarket Class 2 hcap (6f)(1) |
| 17 | 7-304 | **Out Do** D | 8 8-13 | 99-2 | 25-1 | David O'Meara | 3rd Ascot Class 2 hcap (5f) (7) |
| 16 | 40-70 | **Outback Traveller** C, D | 5 9-1 | 100T | 10-1 | Robert Cowell | 4th Ascot Class 2 hcap (7f) (3) |
| 15 | 413-2 | **Interception** D | 5 9-3 | 102-6 | 10-1 | David Lanigan | 2nd Haydock Listed (6f) (0) |
| 14 | 50-22 | **Baccarat** D, BF | 5 9-2 | 105T | 9-1 | Richard Fahey | 2nd York Class 2 hcap (6f) (0) |
| 13 | 56142 | **York Glory** D | 5 9-2 | 100T | 14-1 | Kevin Ryan | 2nd York Class 2 hcap (5f) (0) |

**WINS-RUNS** 3yo 1-0-2, 4yo 2-13-91, 5yo 6-5-65, 6yo+ 1-12-99 **FAVOURITES** -£5.50

**FATE OF FAVOURITES** 0052821039 **POSITION OF WINNER IN MARKET** 6444001940

THIS 1m2f handicap for three-year-olds rated 0-105 was introduced as part of the expanded progamme in 2020 and has been won by 20-1 shot Highland Chief for Paul and Oliver Cole, the Andrew Balding-trained Foxes Tales at 13-2 and last year's 5-2 favourite Missed The Cut for George Boughey.

All three came from double-figure draws in 13- or 14-runner fields, although at least one horse each year has made the first four from the lower half of the draw.

Highland Chief won off top weight from an official rating of 101 but Foxes Tales and Missed The Cut had marks of 93 and 95, and that sort of figure in the low to mid 90s looks ideal from the first three runnings.

Missed The Cut wins last year's Golden Gates Stakes for a delighted George Boughey (below)

This is the longest race of the week at nearly two and three-quarter miles – indeed, the longest run under Flat racing rules – and one of the best loved. With such an emphasis on stamina and with fewer out-and-out stayers in Flat yards nowadays, this race has become quite a battleground between the Flat trainers and the top jumps yards.

## Last year's winner

Stratum made it back-to-back wins at 10-1, even though he did not hit the key trends as well as he had the previous year. He became the fourth dual winner in the past 30 years.

**Form** Most winners had reached a high level over staying distances. Five of the eight different horses to score in the past decade had

### Key trends
▶ *Officially rated 90-plus, 10/10*
▶ *Aged six to nine, 10/10*
▶ *Contested a Group or Listed race since last season, 9/10*
▶ *Top-six finish in race over 2m2f-plus, 8/10*
▶ *Rated within 11lb of RPR top-rated, 8/10*
▶ *Adjusted RPR at least 117, 7/10*

### Other factors
▶ *Only one winner had scored on the Flat that season*

finished in the first four in the Cesarewitch and/or the Northumberland Plate (two had won one of them) and another was a Group 2 Doncaster Cup winner. The others were better known as hurdlers and had won or placed at Grade 2 level.

**Key races** The Chester Cup, Northumberland Plate and the Cesarewitch (plus its trial) are important handicap markers, along with Group races such as the Doncaster Cup, Goodwood Cup and Sagaro Stakes.

**Trainers** Irish champion jumps trainer Willie Mullins made it four wins in the past 11 runnings with Stratum's back-to-back successes and his great Irish rival Gordon Elliott won in 2016 and 2018. On the Flat side Mark Johnston and Andrew Balding both had two winners in the past decade.

Aidan O'Brien runners have to be noted. He won in 2008 with Honolulu and two of his three runners since then have been placed.

**Betting** Twelve of the last 15 winners came from the first four in the market.

## Story of the last ten years

| | FORM | WINNER | AGE & WGT | Adj RPR | SP | TRAINER | BEST RPR LAST 12 MONTHS (RUNS SINCE) |
|---|---|---|---|---|---|---|---|
| 22 | 140-0 | **Stratum** CD | 9 9-7 | 110-14 | 10-1 | Willie Mullins (IRE) | won Queen Alexandra (2m5½f) (3) |
| 21 | 20-15 | **Stratum** | 8 9-2 | 127T | 4-1 | Willie Mullins (IRE) | 2nd Lonsdale Cup Gp2 (2m½f) (3) |
| 20 | 1447- | **Who Dares Wins** | 8 9-2 | 120-1 | Evsf | Alan King | 4th Longchamp Gp1 (2m4f) (1) |
| 19 | 13-36 | **Cleonte** c | 6 9-2 | 120-6 | 7-2 | Andrew Balding | 3rd Sagaro Stakes Gp3 (2m) (1) |
| 18 | 5668- | **Pallasator** c | 9 9-2 | 124-1 | 11-2 | Gordon Elliott (IRE) | 6th Prix Kergorlay Gp2 (1m7f) (1) |
| 17 | 95-25 | **Oriental Fox** CD | 9 9-5 | 117-10 | 10-1 | Mark Johnston | 2nd Newmarket Class 2 hcap (1m6f) (1) |
| 16 | 211/ | **Commissioned** | 6 9-2 | 113-11 | 12-1 | Gordon Elliott (IRE) | Seasonal debut (0) |
| 15 | 3756- | **Oriental Fox** | 7 9-2 | 120-1 | 4-1 | Mark Johnston | 6th Northumberland Plate hcap (2m) (0) |
| 14 | 321-5 | **Pique Sous** | 7 9-2 | 108-18 | 11-4 | Willie Mullins (IRE) | won Leopardstown hcap (1m6f) (1) |
| 13 | 525-5 | **Chiberta King** | 7 9-2 | 119T | 8-1 | Andrew Balding | 5th Goodwood Cup Gp2 (2m) (3) |

**WINS-RUNS:** 4yo 0-6-36, 5yo 0-2-20, 6yo+ 10-12-82 **FAVOURITES:** -£8.00

**TRAINERS IN THIS RACE** (w-pl-r) Willie Mullins 3-4-11, Gordon Elliott 2-1-3, Andrew Balding 2-1-8, Alan King 1-0-6, Charlie Appleby 0-0-2, Aidan O'Brien 0-2-3, Ian Williams 0-4-4, Hughie Morrison 0-0-6, Saeed bin Suroor 0-0-3

**FATE OF FAVOURITES** 2443263197 **POSITION OF WINNER IN MARKET** 4236432125

# EXPERT VIEW Eyecatchers

Racing Post analysts Mark Brown and Richard Young pick a dozen contenders who have grabbed their attention

### ADAYAR

**5yo horse**
**Trainer: Charlie Appleby**

The 2021 Derby and King George winner missed the bulk of the 2022 campaign before squeezing in two quick runs towards the end of the season, including a fine second to Bay Bridge in the Champion Stakes.

He seemed to have retained his powers when winning the rearranged Gordon Richards Stakes at Newmarket on his return and a bold show looks in the offing in the Prince of Wales's Stakes, which could cut up by raceday. (MB)

### AMLETO

**3yo gelding**
**William Haggas**

Amleto is from a family chock-full of winners, most notably 2018 Irish and Yorkshire Oaks winner Sea Of Class, who represented the same connections. After a low-key start to his career, he looked much improved returning from six months off, newly gelded, when easily winning a 1m2½f maiden at Chester's May meeting.

Considering many from William Haggas's yard have needed a run this season, that was a striking effort and a mark of 90 could underestimate him. He looks an ideal type for the King George V Handicap on day three. (MB)

### CICERO'S GIFT

**3yo colt**
**Charlie Hills**

Cicero's Gift has yet to run

> **"Deauville Legend won't mind the drop back to middle distances and it'll be fascinating to see if he can maintain his progress in 2023"**

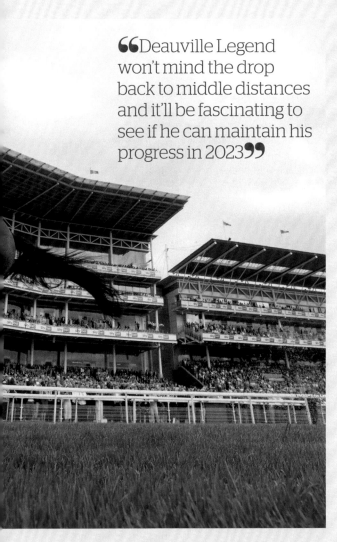

### COLTRANE
**6yo gelding**
**Andrew Balding**

Coltrane thrived during a busy 2022, winning the Doncaster Cup and finishing runner-up in the Lonsdale Cup and at Ascot on Champions Day, and looks to have taken a further step forward this year. His impressive Sagaro Stakes victory on his reappearance makes him a standout candidate for the Gold Cup, especially in the absence of Kyprios.

High class at two miles and with his stamina for the longer test not in doubt, having won last year's Ascot Stakes over course and distance, he has rock-solid claims. (MB)

### DEAUVILLE LEGEND
**4yo gelding**
**James Ferguson**

After a gelding operation in late 2021, Deauville Legend made rapid strides during a three-year-old career that saw him win the Group 2 Great Voltigeur and finish a fine fourth in the Melbourne Cup.

Although the Flemington race was over 2m on soft ground, he won't mind the drop back to middle distances and it'll be fascinating to see if he can maintain his progress in 2023. His trainer reports he has done well over the winter and is on course to run in the Hardwicke. (RY)

in a Pattern race and his name may still be relatively unknown to some, but that could be about to change.

The 2,000 Guineas result, with huge outsiders rated in the 90s finishing second and fourth, suggested there's room for a horse out of left-field to make his claim in the three-year-old miling division, and this son of Muhaarar has done nothing but impress in winning his three starts.

His latest Goodwood win showed off his turn of foot and it would be no surprise to see a big run in the St James's Palace Stakes. (MB)

# EXPERT VIEW Eyecatchers

## DOCKLANDS

**3yo colt**
**Harry Eustace**

Harry Eustace had his first Royal Ascot winner last year with Latin Lover in the Palace of Holyroodhouse Handicap and Docklands is a strong candidate for a more prestigious success in the Britannia. It's a notoriously competitive handicap but Docklands looks tailor-made for it, having gained experience of the straight mile at Ascot when bolting up on his handicap debut in May.

His earlier Wolverhampton form with St James's Palace contender Cicero's Gift, now rated 109, suggests a 14lb rise, taking him to a mark of 94, is well within his scope. He looks set to run a big race granted a bit of luck with the draw and regular rider Hayley Turner is better than most on the straight mile. (MB)

## FIRST OF MAY

**3yo filly**
**James Fanshawe**

Having improved significantly with each run, First Of May is a handicapper with plenty of upside. A combination of inexperience and heavy ground were likely the main factors for her debut defeat but she has since won twice over 6f on Tapeta.

Her handicap debut at Wolverhampton in early May was impressive, barely coming off the bridle to beat a reliable yardstick and shaping as though a drop to 5f wouldn't inconvenience her. The Palace of Holyroodhouse Handicap could be the perfect next step. (RY)

## HIS MAJESTY

**2yo colt**
**Aidan O'Brien**

His Majesty, who could almost have been named with this meeting in mind, looks a high-quality juvenile with an attitude to match judged on his successful debut at the Curragh in early May. The imposing son of No Nay Never was green when asked for his effort but stuck on resolutely.

Although not as flashy as stable companion River Tiber, who won his debut by a wide margin at Navan, he is the type to improve and quicker ground shouldn't be a problem. He'll be suited by 6f and the Coventry looks the ideal race. (RY)

## MONTASSIB

**5yo gelding**
**William Haggas**

Montassib confirmed the promise of his previous Haydock run when breaking

a losing run of a year at Newmarket in May, looking better than the bare form in a muddling event, and he appeals for one of the week's big handicaps.

A stiffer test of his stamina at Ascot's more galloping track will be ideal and he will appeal in either the Buckingham Palace (fifth last year) over 7f or the Royal Hunt Cup over a mile. (RY)

Peking Opera: primed for a big run in the Queen's Vase

bombed out on ground considered "too tacky" in first-time cheekpieces at Newmarket on 2,000 Guineas day, showed that to be all wrong on quicker ground in a 6f handicap at York's Dante meeting, staying on well at the end having been tapped for toe.

Ascot's stiffer course should be much more to his liking and, given he's unexposed as a sprinter, he'll make a fair bit of each-way appeal in the Wokingham granted a sound surface. (RY)

## WELLINGTON
### 7yo gelding
### Richard Gibson

Wellington has been 16-1 in ante-post betting for the Queen Elizabeth II Jubilee Stakes but is unlikely to be so big on raceday.

Last season's champion sprinter in Hong Kong has had the misfortune to bump into a rampant Lucky Sweynesse this term, although he got the better of his adversary in the Hong Kong Sprint in December.

Trainer Richard Gibson saddled Gold-Fun to be second in this race in 2016 and Wellington appeals in a division lacking an outstanding performer. (RY)

## PEKING OPERA
### 3yo colt
### Aidan O'Brien

Having won a mile Leopardstown maiden on his second and final start as a juvenile, Peking Opera took a good step forward when landing the Listed Yeats Stakes over 1m5f at Navan in mid-May, overcoming a modest gallop to assert late.

Clearly a strong stayer, the son of Galileo was put forward as a likely Queen's Vase type by connections, who have won five of the last ten runnings. He is set to head there primed to run another career-best. (MB)

## SPIRIT OF LIGHT
### 6yo gelding
### Ian Williams

Spirit Of Light, who

ROYAL ASCOT enters a new era this year with the first meeting to be held in the reign of King Charles III. He becomes the 13th monarch in the occasion's long history, which dates back to Queen Anne and her vision for a racecourse on the heath in 1711.

The wheel of change moves slowly at Royal Ascot and the long-standing traditions will remain in place.

There will be all the familiar sights (from the royal procession to the famous greencoats) and sounds (from the national anthem before racing to the bandstand singalong afterwards).

The difference this year will be that the focus is on King Charles and Queen Camilla. They will be in the first carriage of the royal procession and have leading roles in the trophy presentations.

Global interest in the new king is high in the afterglow of his coronation and that will bring one of racing's showpiece occasions into the spotlight. Charles and Camilla at Royal Ascot will be on newspaper front pages and news bulletins around the world, giving racing a special kind of exposure to a huge audience.

At the start of each day cameras will focus on the royal procession, which brings the monarch and his guests along the straight mile in horse-drawn carriages, parading in front of the vast crowds before turning under the grandstand and into the parade ring.

The origins of the procession go back to 1825 during the reign of King George IV. Charles will be the ninth monarch to take part in the tradition. Initially the procession took place on only one day of the

The royal procession ends in the parade ring each afternoon

**10.30AM** The famous Greencoats open the gates to signal the start of the day.

**2PM** The royal procession starts at the top of the course, passing each of the enclosures in its journey along the straight mile.

**2.30PM** Racing gets under way at the same time every day.

**6.10PM** The scheduled start time for the last of the seven races on the recently expanded programme.

**6.40PM** A much-loved communal singalong as the Band of the Grenadier Guards plays a selection of classics in the Queen Anne Enclosure.

**8PM/9PM** The day draws to a close at 8pm in the Royal, Queen Anne and Windsor Enclosures, while on Thursday, Friday and Saturday the party in the Village Enclosure continues until 9pm.

meeting before it was extended to all days in 1919, in celebration of victory in the First World War.

The procession starts not by carriage but by car. The King and his guests will leave Windsor Castle at 1.35pm and be driven by car to the Ascot Gate of Windsor Great Park, where they will transfer to four horse-drawn carriages.

Each landau carriage carries four people, with the King at the head of the group. The carriages are pulled by Windsor greys and bays, mainly Cleveland bays, who are trained as carriage horses from the age of four and work for approximately 15 years.

The procession along the straight mile starts at 2pm precisely and a different path is chosen each day, to protect the ground. As the procession reaches the grandstand, the national anthem is played by a guards band.

A celebratory start to the day and a welcome fit for a king.

# ROYAL ASCOT A rich legacy

QUEEN ELIZABETH II will be remembered at Royal Ascot this year – and with good reason. This meeting, and racing in general, owes a huge debt of gratitude to the longest-reigning monarch, who did so much to advance the sport's standing.

The Platinum Jubilee Stakes, held on the final day of the meeting on June 24, has been renamed in perpetuity as The Queen Elizabeth II Jubilee Stakes. Long known as the Cork and Orrery Stakes, the race was renamed three times this century in commemoration of her Golden, Diamond and Platinum Jubilees.

"The Queen had so much success at Royal Ascot and we thought it was appropriate to specifically rename a race in her honour," Ascot's director of racing Nick Smith said. "While we also have the Queen Elizabeth II Stakes on Champions Day named after her, she had so many winners at Royal Ascot and was such a major part of the meeting.

"Alongside the Gold Cup this was the race she traditionally presented for and it was the logical race to choose. Since 2002 the contest has always honoured her for her jubilee achievements and now it honours her whole life."

Right up to her death on September 8 last year, the Queen was absorbed by the sport she loved. Royal Ascot's five days, along with Derby day, were always the first marked in her diary each year. She first attended the meeting as a 19-year-old in 1945 and hardly missed a day after acceding to the throne in 1952.

Her passion for racing took its most high-profile days to a wider audience and helped to maintain its standing as an important part of the sporting landscape. Undoubtedly she was a big draw for the overseas owners and trainers who have helped to transform Royal Ascot into a truly international event in the 21st century.

The Queen left a huge legacy, both in her own right as a high-profile owner-breeder and in a wider context as a passionate supporter and benefactor. She was champion owner twice and won all the British Classics except the Derby, in which she had runner-up Aureole, and earned a reputation as the most knowledgeable and most enthusiastic of all the monarchs who have ever been involved in racing.

This was a week that held a special place in her affections and brought her

Queen Elizabeth II will be commemorated by the renaming of Saturday's Group 1 sprint

so much success and happiness. Never more so than in 2013 when she won the treasured Gold Cup with her brave mare Estimate. In all she had 76 winners at Ascot (72 on the Flat, four over jumps), including 24 at the royal meeting.

The famous royal colours of purple, scarlet and gold silk, which the Queen inherited from her father, King George VI, will race on. They will continue to be a symbol of a rich royal history at this most special of race meetings.

## THE QUEEN'S 24 ROYAL ASCOT WINNERS

| YEAR | RACE | HORSE | JOCKEY |
| --- | --- | --- | --- |
| 1953 | Royal Hunt Cup | **CHOIR BOY** | Doug Smith |
| 1954 | Hardwicke Stakes | **AUREOLE** | Eph Smith |
| | Rous Memorial Stakes | **LANDAU** | Gordon Richards |
| 1955 | King George V Stakes | **JARDINIERE** | Doug Smith |
| 1956 | Royal Hunt Cup | **ALEXANDER** | Harry Carr |
| 1957 | Ribblesdale Stakes | **ALMERIA** | Harry Carr |
| | New Stakes | **PALL MALL** | Harry Carr |
| 1958 | Rous Memorial Stakes | **SNOW CAT** | Eph Smith |
| | King Edward VII Stakes | **RESTORATION** | Harry Carr |
| 1959 | St James's Palace Stakes | **ABOVE SUSPICION** | Harry Carr |
| | King Edward VII Stakes | **PINDARI** | Lester Piggott |
| 1961 | Coronation Stakes | **AIMING HIGH** | Lester Piggott |
| 1968 | Hardwicke Stakes | **HOPEFUL VENTURE** | Sandy Barclay |
| 1970 | Ascot Stakes | **MAGNA CARTA** | Geoff Lewis |
| 1979 | Queen's Vase | **BUTTRESS** | Willie Carson |
| | Ribblesdale Stakes | **EXPANSIVE** | Willie Carson |
| 1992 | Royal Hunt Cup | **COLOUR SERGEANT** | David Harrison |
| 1995 | Ribblesdale Stakes | **PHANTOM GOLD** | Frankie Dettori |
| 1999 | Duke of Edinburgh Stakes | **BLUEPRINT** | Gary Stevens |
| 2008 | Chesham Stakes | **FREE AGENT** | Richard Hughes |
| 2012 | Queen's Vase | **ESTIMATE** | Ryan Moore |
| 2013 | Gold Cup | **ESTIMATE** | Ryan Moore |
| 2016 | Hardwicke Stakes | **DARTMOUTH** | Olivier Peslier |
| 2020 | Windsor Castle Stakes | **TACTICAL** | James Doyle |

**❝Racing is doubly lucky to have both the King and the Queen Consort. The King always said he was going to take it seriously and everything he's done since he inherited the stock has been true to his word❞**

ONE of the first visits made by the King following his coronation on May 6 was to Newmarket, where he inspected the horses he has in training in joint-ownership with Queen Camilla.

It was a deeply symbolic visit that continued an annual tradition of his mother and reaffirmed his commitment to carrying on the strong royal ties with horseracing. His presence at Royal Ascot as the new monarch will be the most potent signal of all.

In his visit to Newmarket, the King had a private tour of the four stables he supports – John and Thady Gosden, Sir Michael Stoute, William Haggas and Sir Mark Prescott – and which house some of the horses who may don his colours at Royal Ascot.

Among the team of seven the King was shown at the Gosdens' Clarehaven base was Saga, who went close to registering a royal success on coronation day when beaten a head in the Suffolk Handicap at

Newmarket. The grey also lost by the same margin in last year's Britannia Handicap at Royal Ascot, denying Queen Elizabeth II a winner at what was her last Royal Ascot.

Saga will have long been pencilled in for the royal meeting again and has been joined on the list recently by three-year-old stablemate Slipofthepen. He was the first winner jointly for Charles and Camilla when he took a mile conditions race at Kempton on April 10. The

Haggas-trained Blue Missile and Desert Hero are other possible runners.

They are among about 100 thoroughbred horses inherited by King Charles from his mother. The depth of the legacy is emphasised by the fact that Slipofthepen comes from a family that goes back eight generations within the Royal Studs.

Charles does not have the same innate understanding of the thoroughbred as his mother but he is committed to continuing her good work alongside Camilla, who has a keen and long-standing interest in racing.

"Racing is doubly lucky to have both the King and the Queen Consort who very much want to engage," says John Warren, the royal racing and bloodstock adviser.

"The King always said he was going to take it seriously and everything he's done since he inherited the stock has been true to his word.

"He wants to reap as much information as he can so he knows the subject significantly better than the osmosis of knowing it at arm's length, but obviously that's been tremendously helped by the fact the Queen Consort has a fundamental interest in horses anyway."

The excitement of a Royal Ascot winner would undoubtedly boost their interest immensely. With several royal runners in the offing, this could be the year for a special first.

# The Royal Ascot Lookbook

## Ascot showcases a fresh approach to styling and sartorial elegance

This year sees the launch of the Royal Ascot Lookbook, replacing the Style Guide that has been running for the past decade or so. While the official dress code remains unchanged, the idea behind the Lookbook is to offer inspiration across the Royal Enclosure, Queen Anne Enclosure and Village Enclosure, encouraging racegoers to dream up an outfit that is authentic to their personal style and approach to sartorial shopping.

The Lookbook comprises six fashion edits: luxe, tailoring, pre-loved and rental, vintage, high street and emerging designer.

Partnering with leading stylist Luke Jefferson Day and photographer Damian Foxe, Ascot aims to encapsulate occasionwear dressing for the spring/summer 2023 season.

Day says: "This season I wanted to inspire racegoers to be a little more unconventional and inventive in the way they dress up, and how they source their looks. We've championed innovative British designers, while also showcasing international brands from further afield. I want to excite people to think outside of the box – whether that be shopping resourcefully on the high street or by being more eco-conscious through hiring a look or finding a rare vintage gem."

Words and pictures by kind permission of Ascot

# Style Guide

## THE KEY POINTS

### ROYAL ENCLOSURE

**Ladies**

- Formal daywear is a requirement
- Dresses and skirts should fall just above the knee or longer
- Shoulder straps must have a minimum width of one inch
- Trouser suits and jumpsuits are welcome – trouser suits should be full length, of matching material and colour; jumpsuits should fall below the knee and comply with the shoulder strap requirements
- Hats must be worn. Headpieces must have a solid base of four inches or more in diameter

**Gentlemen**

- Black, grey or navy morning dress
- With a waistcoat and tie (no cravats, bow ties or neckerchiefs)
- A black or grey top hat
- Black shoes with socks

### QUEEN ANNE ENCLOSURE

**Ladies**

- Ladies are required to dress for a formal daytime occasion
- A hat, headpiece or fascinator should be worn
- Strapless or sheer dresses and tops are not permitted
- Trouser suits must be full-length and jumpsuits should fall below the knee
- Shorts are not permitted

**Gentlemen**

- A full-length suit with a collared shirt and tie must be worn (no cravats, bow ties or neckerchiefs)
- Jackets and trousers should be of matching material
- Socks must be worn and should cover the ankle

### VILLAGE ENCLOSURE

**Ladies**

- Ladies are required to dress for a formal daytime occasion

- A hat, headpiece or fascinator should be worn at all times
- Strapless or sheer dresses and tops are not permitted
- Trouser suits must be full-length and jumpsuits should fall below the knee
- Shorts are not permitted

**Gentlemen**

- A suit jacket or blazer, full-length trousers or chinos, collared shirt and tie must be worn
- Ties, bow ties and cravats can be worn
- Socks must be worn and should cover the ankle
- Jeans, trainers and shorts are not permitted

### WINDSOR ENCLOSURE

No official dress code, but ladies and gentlemen are encouraged to dress in smart daywear. It is recommended that ladies wear smart attire with a hat, headpiece or fascinator and gentlemen a jacket and collared shirt

What the Lookbook says: Featuring soft, buttery silk gowns by Roksanda, velvet mirrored suiting by Gucci and perfectly paired three-piece morning dress by Favourbrook, the luxe edit showcases a reimagined approach to designer dressing.

# FASHION

**High street**

What the Lookbook says: Depicting style that transcends 'off the peg' suit buying, the high street edit sparks intrigue in summer linens, mint tailoring, alternative prints and glamorous dresses suitable for all enclosures. Featured brands include LK Bennett, Sandro, All Saints and Reformation.

# The looks

### Tailoring

What the Lookbook says: Taking pleats and darts to the next level, the immaculate tailoring is here to make a statement in the Lookbook. With daring colour block suits, contemporary soft shades and traditional fine tailoring, the tailoring edit presents inspiration from Zimmermann, Edward Sexton and RXQUETTE.

### Vintage

What the Lookbook says: Complete with sleek 1980s skirt suits by Thierry Mugler, preppy blazers by Vivienne Westwood and flamboyant fuchsia silhouettes, the vintage edit evokes a sleek and surprisingly modern aesthetic for raceday styling, inherited from iconic wardrobes of yesteryear.

# FASHION

# The looks

### Pre-loved and rental

What the Lookbook says: With sustainable dressing at the forefront of the style agenda, the pre-loved and rental edit showcases spectacular second-hand and hireable fashion from leaders in the rental space including HURR, Selfridges Rental, Moss Bros and Oliver Brown. From raiding grandma's hat boxes to scouring charity shops for treasures, this edit is for the sartorially adventurous who are after unique fashion finds.

### Emerging designer

What the Lookbook says: Celebrating looks from the most coveted up-and-coming fashion designers. Luke pairs a billowing S.S. Daley checked suit with epic dream catcher-inspired millinery crafted by Victoria Grant. Never-before-included designers Richard Quinn, Charles Jeffery LOVERBOY and Ahluwalia are heralded in the emerging designer edit.

FAIRFAX & FAVOR

ENGLAND

*Pioneering Rural Vogue*

FAIRFAXANDFAVOR.COM

# Big opener for Frankie

THE effervescent Frankie Dettori is synonymous with Ascot and there is a favourite's chance the legendary rider can kick off his final royal meeting with a record-extending eighth victory in the Queen Anne Stakes aboard Inspiral.

Dettori has another leading chance on the opening day with 2,000 Guineas winner Chaldean in the St James's Palace Stakes but first the sport's most famous jockey will be keen to start on the right note with Cheveley Park Stud's star filly.

Inspiral was the highlight of what was an otherwise disappointing Royal Ascot for Dettori and John and Thady Gosden last year – she was their only winner in a week that had more lows for the jockey-trainer partnership.

Dettori was criticised by Gosden snr for his ride on star stayer Stradivarius in the Gold Cup, while he also made a mess of removing the hood from Lord North in the Prince of Wales's Stakes and finished second aboard royal runners Saga in the Britannia Handicap and Reach For The Moon in the Hampton Court Stakes.

Class is permanent, however, and Dettori bounced back on Inspiral in the Coronation Stakes for an impressive near five-length success on her first start at the track.

Similarities can be drawn between her preparation then and now. Inspiral was ante-post favourite for last year's 1,000 Guineas after a perfect four-race juvenile campaign but missed the Classic after her training "had not been 100 per cent straightforward".

Just five days before this year's expected reappearance in the Lockinge Stakes, connections revealed they were not entirely happy with her progress and favoured heading straight to Royal Ascot. On last year's showing, that could be a positive.

Inspiral recorded her best Racing Post Rating in the Coronation – her figure was bettered only by 2018 winner Alpha Centauri in the past decade – but her season was somewhat up and down.

It was felt she ran flat when a beaten 1-7 favourite in second behind Prosperous Voyage in the Falmouth Stakes at Newmarket before she gained another top-level win in the Prix Jacques le Marois at Deauville.

All that could go wrong did go wrong when she was a never-nearer sixth in the

Inspiral and Frankie Dettori before winning last year's Coronation Stakes

Queen Elizabeth II Stakes at Ascot in October – a slow start and a muddling gallop put paid to her chances – but she might just be best fresh in the summer.

If that is the case, Inspiral could join Dettori's illustrious list of Queen Anne winners that includes Markofdistinction, Refuse To Bend and Palace Pier.

## STAR RATING
★★★★★

Owner: Cheveley Park Stud
Trainers: John & Thady Gosden

**❝Inspiral could join Dettori's illustrious list of Queen Anne winners❞**

# Newmarket hero

FINDING the key formlines is essential for any race but it is usually a straightforward task when it comes to the St James's Palace Stakes – just look back at the 2,000 Guineas.

Five of the seven 2,000 Guineas winners to have contested this race in the past decade were successful, including Coroebus last year, and the two Classic scorers to have been beaten in this period – Night Of Thunder and Churchill – suffered reverses against horses they had defeated in the Guineas in Kingman and Barney Roy.

Chaldean was this year's 2,000 Guineas hero, maintaining a prominent position under Frankie Dettori and keeping on best in soft ground to beat 125-1 outsider Hi Royal, but was it a stellar renewal?

Racing Post Ratings awarded Chaldean a figure of 120 – just 2lb higher than his Dewhurst win over Royal Scotsman last year and the

joint-lowest rating for a Guineas winner in the past ten years.

It is not all bad news as the other 120-rated winner was Poetic Flare, who went on to land the St James's Palace – following runs in the French and Irish 2,000 Guineas – in 2021.

While our RPR team felt he showed marginal improvement on his best two-year-old form, connections took a different view.

Barry Mahon, Juddmonte's racing manager, said: "He was good last year but, jeez, he's better this year. He's a son of Frankel, a Group 1-winning two-year-old and a Classic-winning three-year-old. You can't get much better than that."

Unseating his rider at the start of the Greenham on his first start at three proved no hindrance to Chaldean's Classic bid and the Andrew Balding-trained colt has a particularly likeable attitude.

Chaldean has yet to race around a bend, and the closest he has come to experiencing such a racing style was when he was successful in the Acomb Stakes at York, where the seven-furlong start is in a chute and the runners take a slight left turn to enter the home straight.

He beat Indestructible by half a length that day before defeating the same rival by three and a half lengths in the Champagne at Doncaster on his next start and almost 13 lengths in the Guineas.

Chaldean may have simply improved considerably since York but, given he is such a stout stayer, an end-to-end gallop on a straight course may well suit him better than this test.

## STAR RATING

★ ★ ★ ★

Chaldean is a top chance for Frankie Dettori after their 2,000 Guineas triumph

# Tiny, tough, talented

THE 1,000 Guineas winner has more often than not gone on to contest the Coronation Stakes in the past decade and the obvious target for Mawj after her Classic success is an attempt to become the third filly since 2013 to complete the Newmarket-Royal Ascot double.

Sky Lantern and Winter were the two to do it recently, while Hermosa finished second in the Coronation, Mother Earth was third and Billesdon Brook, a shock Guineas winner in 2018, finished fourth. Last year's Classic heroine Cachet fared worst in fifth.

Mawj had been fairly well touted for the 1,000 Guineas on the back of a fruitful two-year-old campaign, including victory in the Group 2 Duchess of Cambridge Stakes on the July course, and a 2-2 record when stepped up to seven furlongs and a mile at Meydan over the winter.

However, by the time Guineas weekend came around in early May, the feeling was the rain-softened ground had gone against the Godolphin filly. She proved that theory to be wide of the mark.

Mawj was ridden positively by Oisin Murphy and came under pressure before favourite Tahiyra. She showed a fine attitude, however, to repel that rival by half a length, and the fact they were seven and a half lengths clear of the third suggests the first two are particularly talented fillies.

Her victory was a first in a British Classic for Saeed bin Suroor since Mastery landed the 2009 St Leger. The trainer said: "She's a tiny filly but has a big heart. Her pedigree has plenty of speed, but we tried her over a mile in Dubai and she got it well."

Mawj may not have the same scope for improvement as other Guineas winners, but if she were to run to a similar level at Royal Ascot, she would be a big player.

She was a beaten favourite in the Albany at last year's meeting but ran creditably in finishing second to Meditate, who was only sixth in the 1,000 Guineas.

The Albany was run on good to firm, as were Mawj's two victories as a juvenile, but two of her three wins this year have been on soft ground, so while she may prove to be at her best on a sounder surface, she is clearly versatile.

## STAR RATING
★ ★ ★ ★

Owner: Godolphin
Trainer: Saeed bin Suroor

Classic glory for Mawj in
the 1,000 Guineas

113

# Globetrotting miler now a serious player

William Buick celebrates victory on Modern Games at the Breeders' Cup (facing page)

CHARLIE APPLEBY has saddled only two runners in the Queen Anne Stakes but set his sights on a breakthrough victory in the Royal Ascot curtain-raiser as far back as November.

"The Queen Anne is the obvious aim next year," said the Godolphin trainer after Modern Games had struck at the Breeders' Cup for the second year in a row.

Modern Games landed the Juvenile Turf at Del Mar in 2021 and followed up at the big international meeting when winning the Mile at Keeneland – a race that included Prix de la Foret and British Champions Sprint scorer Kinross and 2020 winner Order Of Australia.

The four-year-old has a 3-4 record on firm ground in the US and Canada, and two of those runs were his best efforts on Racing Post Ratings until he produced a career high of 124 with a length-and-a-half victory in the Group 1 Lockinge Stakes on good ground at Newbury in May.

That made it clear Appleby's plan was coming together nicely. It was also a resounding riposte to those who had questioned Modern Games's CV because most of the prominent entries were gained outside Britain.

"That's his fifth Group/ Grade 1 win now, but his first in England, which is

what I think everyone was waiting to see," the trainer said at Newbury. "It was an important day for him. To do that on home soil is a big feather in his cap."

Modern Games's other European Group 1 win came in last year's French 2,000 Guineas, at a time when he appeared to be down the Godolphin pecking order behind Coroebus and Native Trail, who finished one-two in the Newmarket Guineas.

Consistency became his watchword with solid placed efforts in the Prix du Jockey Club, Sussex Stakes and Queen Elizabeth II Stakes, but all without getting into the 120s on RPRs in Europe.

That changed emphatically with his Lockinge victory, making him the one to beat in the Queen Anne. "He's a top-class miler – end of," was jockey William Buick's pithy verdict at Newbury.

Dry weather will be key to Modern Games's chance. Despite winning the French 2,000 on good to soft, he has a 1-4 record in such conditions, extending to 3-8 on good ground or easier even with his Lockinge win.

In favourable conditions, however, Appleby will have a great chance to start the meeting with a bang.

## STAR RATING
★ ★ ★ ★ ★

# Fairytale princess

> **❝She always comes on for her first run and the King's Stand is her next target. She's got speed to burn❞**

THE King's Stand market is largely dominated by sprinters aged three or four but recent trends suggest older horses warrant the utmost respect.

Five of the last ten scorers have been aged six or above, including 2022 ace Nature Strip, with just three winners aged three or four in the past decade.

Highfield Princess turned six this year and has a wonderful rags-to-riches story. She started off in handicaps with an official mark of 57 in August 2020 and, less than a year later, won the Buckingham Palace Handicap at the royal meeting off 92.

That victory came over seven furlongs but the John Quinn-trained mare has excelled since being dropped to sprint distances. She secured a hat-trick of top-level wins last summer in the Prix Maurice de Gheest, Nunthorpe and Flying Five and ended the campaign with a fourth in the Breeders' Cup Turf Sprint.

Her return this season suggested she has lost none of her ability. She might even have improved.

Carrying a 5lb penalty for her Flying Five win, Highfield Princess gave weight away all round in the Duke of York Stakes but ran a mighty race to finish a half-length second to Azure Blue.

Quinn said: "Nobody knows from year to year whether a horse will retain its ability and she was a mare going from five to six but she showed all her enthusiasm. She always comes on for her first run and will be running in Group 1s now and won't have a penalty. The King's Stand is her next target. She's got speed to burn."

Highfield Princess recorded her joint-second-highest Racing Post Rating on her return, equalling her Flying Five RPR and just 2lb shy of her career-best in the Nunthorpe.

Winning Group 1s on ground ranging from good to firm to soft last year proved her versatility with conditions and she is a strong stayer over the minimum distance given one of her top-level wins came over six and a half furlongs.

Despite winning at Royal Ascot, one slight concern is her record at the track. She has been beaten in three subsequent visits, including when sixth in the Champions Sprint in 2021 and the Platinum Jubilee last year.

This will be her first start over the minimum distance at Ascot, however, and on her York showing there is every chance her fairytale story can continue.

## STAR RATING
★ ★ ★ ★ ★

## Cicero's Gift

Owner: Rosehill Racing
Trainer: Charlie Hills

# Attitude and ability

THE normal route to the St James's Palace Stakes is via a Guineas and it's a path that was considered for Cicero's Gift before Charlie Hills decided a Classic test would be too much too soon for his exciting colt.

Instead Cicero's Gift was pointed towards the St James's Palace off a less taxing preparation more in the mould of recent John Gosden-trained winners Without Parole and Palace Pier.

Neither had set foot in a Group race before Royal Ascot, let alone a Group 1, and that will also be the case for Cicero's Gift. The day before the 2,000 Guineas, he headed to Goodwood for a conditions race over a mile and won so impressively that Hills immediately looked towards the St James's Palace.

"It was pleasing to see him take the step up in grade in his stride," the trainer said in his William Hill blog. "It was the first time he really

had to put his head down and race properly, so it was fantastic that he showed the ability I've been pretty confident was there. He's a very exciting horse."

His Goodwood victory by five and a half lengths followed novice wins at Newbury in October and Wolverhampton in March. A Racing Post Rating of 112 was a big step up and, while it leaves him with 8lb to find on Guineas winner Chaldean, the gap to the top level is bridgeable.

By comparison, Without Parole and Palace Pier had RPRs of 111 and 110 when they headed to the St James's Palace.

As a talented son of Hills's champion sprinter Muhaarar, Cicero's Gift was always likely to find a place in his trainer's heart. "He's a smashing-looking horse, very imposing like his dad was, and he's got a great attitude," Hills said.

Royal Ascot was where Muhaarar burst on to the Group 1 scene with a stunning victory in the inaugural Commonwealth Cup in 2015. Like father, like son? Hills hopes so.

## STAR RATING
★★★

# Horseboxes – Uprating and Downplating

## Uprating Horseboxes

As you may be aware, the DVSA is paying close attention to the horsebox industry and in particular, to lightweight horseboxes which they suspect may be operating overweight.

We have seen cases of horseboxes being stopped, checked and impounded on the roadside, owing to running overweight. The horses in transit have to be loaded into a different box and taken away, and the resultant fines are ever increasing in size. Yet, there is an alternative.

SvTech is keen to promote its uprating service for lightweight horseboxes (3500kg), whereby the horsebox can gain an extra 200-300kg in payload. This provides vital payload capability when carrying an extra horse and/or tack and offers peace of mind for the owner.

SvTech has carried out extensive work and testing on lightweight models and has covered uprates for most lightweight vehicles.

It is worth noting that some uprates require modifications or changes to the vehicle's braking, tyres and/or suspension, for which SvTech provides a simple

purpose-built suspension assister kit. This will take between 1-2 hours for you to fit. Your horsebox will then go for a formal inspection to bring it into the 'Goods' category, and, depending on the vehicle's age, may also require fitment of a speed limiter, for which there are one or two options. Most importantly, vehicles registered after May 2002 must be fitted with manufacturer's ABS, if going above 3500kg.

If you're unsure, or don't believe that you need to uprate your lightweight horsebox, try taking it to a public weighbridge when you're fully loaded with your horse, tack, passenger, hay, etc. and weigh off each axle individually and the vehicle as a whole. There could be a distinct chance that you've overloaded one of the axles, even if you're within the GVW. If there is a problem, we can help. Call us to discuss your options.

## Downplating Horseboxes

Do you own a 10 - 12.5 tonnes horsebox and do you want non-HGV licence holder to drive it? Your horsebox could be downplated to 7.5 tonnes so that any driver with a licence issued prior to 1st Jan 1997 could drive it.

- You are paying too much Vehicle Excise Duty.
- You want to escape the need for a tachograph.

The most important aspect when downplating is to leave yourself suitable payload to carry your goods. The Ministry requires that for horseboxes of 7500kg there is a minimum payload of 2000kg. Hence, when downplating to 7500kg, the unladen weight must not exceed 5500kg. For 3500kg horseboxes, you must ensure that you have a payload of at least 1000kg, thus, when empty it cannot weigh more than 2500kg.

Due to recent changes at DVSA, we are no longer required to make a mechanical change to the vehicle and, once downrated, we will be supplying you with a revised set of Ministry plating certificates, or if exempt, plating and testing, a converter's plate and certificate at the lower weight.

Depending upon vehicle usage, it is at the discretion of DVSA as to whether they will require a formal inspection of your vehicle.

TO DISCOVER YOUR OPTIONS, PLEASE DOWNLOAD, FILL IN AND RETURN OUR ENQUIRY FORM – WWW.SVTECH.CO.UK

# Royal appointment

THE score may be two-nil to 2,000 Guineas hero Chaldean but there are reasons to believe Royal Scotsman could turn the tables in the St James's Palace Stakes.

Royal Scotsman was beaten just a head by Chaldean in the Dewhurst at the back end of last season *(below)* and third place in the first Classic of the season could certainly be marked up.

Jim Crowley's mount pulled notably hard in the early stages, forfeited some ground when receiving a bump after two furlongs and made his challenge away from the first two home.

The considerable ease underfoot was likely not in his favour either, although Oliver Cole, who trains Royal Scotsman with his father Paul, felt there were no excuses and took plenty of encouragement from the run.

Cole jnr said: "He's run a massive race to be third but was a bit too keen in the early stages. He had no problem with the ground as he goes on anything. It was always the idea to come straight here and hopefully he can improve from this and we can have another crack at the winner at Royal Ascot."

**❝Hopefully he can improve from this and we can have another crack at the winner at Royal Ascot❞**

While Royal Scotsman, a Goodwood novice winner on good to soft last year, may be able to handle variations of ground, his best performances came on a quicker surface at two, including when justifying odds-on favouritism in the Group 2 Richmond Stakes at Glorious Goodwood.

A dry lead-up to the royal meeting would aid his chance and the St James's Palace might just be run to suit him better than Chaldean.

Royal Scotsman travels well through his races and possesses a good turn of foot – two assets that could be crucial as he goes around a bend for the first time on Ascot's Old Mile. There is more potential for a stop-start gallop around a bend and, while that could be a negative for Chaldean, it could favour the nippier Royal Scotsman.

Another tick in the box for Royal Scotsman is his course experience, having finished fourth at Ascot on his debut last year before placing third in the Coventry Stakes behind Bradsell at the royal meeting.

Mark Brown, who analysed the 2,000 Guineas for the Racing Post, wrote: "All told, Royal Scotsman ran a massive race and connections will no doubt fancy their chances of reversing the form at Royal Ascot."

There is plenty to suggest he could do just that.

## STAR RATING
★ ★ ★

Royal Scotsman powers home at Goodwood last summer

# Ascot form a big plus

Adayar: promising
reappearance win

THE Prince of Wales's Stakes may be a first start at the royal meeting for Adayar but it is his Ascot form that marks him out as a leading contender.

The Godolphin five-year-old's top Racing Post Rating of 128 was recorded when winning the King George over 1m4f at the track in 2021. His stamina was an asset that day but he has predominantly been campaigned over this 1m2f trip since.

Adayar's joint-second-highest RPR – alongside his Derby win in 2021 – came when a half-length runner-up in the Champion Stakes at Ascot last October.

He was beaten by Bay Bridge that day and they are set to clash for a second time in this fascinating top-level contest.

There were no excuses for Adayar in the Champion Stakes but it was just his second, and final, start of an interrupted campaign, having missed the Coronation Cup and a defence of the King George due to setbacks.

Adayar had finished fifth in the previous year's Champion Stakes and Racing Post Ratings confirmed his second attempt was a much-improved effort, raising hope that he is capable of a coveted Group 1 success at a mile and a quarter.

That view was enhanced on his reappearance on 1,000 Guineas day at Newmarket in May. Although he faced just four rivals in the Gordon Richards Stakes (saved from Sandown's cancelled meeting in late April), it was no gimme with the progressive Anmaat among his opposition.

Adayar cleared away for a two-and-a-half-length success, with trainer Charlie Appleby taking plenty of positives from the performance.

Appleby said: "William Buick said it was tiring ground and he didn't handle the Dip but good horses can overcome all those negatives.

"I've always wanted to get Adayar a Group 1 over a mile and a quarter because I think it will look good on his CV. Better ground will suit him better and we'll get a nice, strong pace to run at in the Prince of Wales's, which will suit him down to the ground, and we know he loves Ascot."

Adayar has run only twice on good ground or quicker and the soundest surface he has encountered was when winning the King George on good to firm. If similar conditions prevail on day two of Royal Ascot, a big performance could be forthcoming.

## STAR RATING
★ ★ ★ ★ ★

> 66Better ground will suit him better and we'll get a nice, strong pace to run at in the Prince of Wales's99

# Turning back the clock

DAZZLING at three but disappointing at four, Hurricane Lane was kept around as a five-year-old this season in the hope that he could recapture the 2021 form that brought Classic success in the Irish Derby and St Leger.

There was an early positive sign in his Group 2 Jockey Club Stakes victory at Newmarket's Guineas meeting and perhaps there will be another at Royal Ascot in the Hardwicke Stakes. With trainer Charlie Appleby adamant he is working back from the Prix de l'Arc de Triomphe with his fallen star, the royal meeting could be an important staging post.

Last year's Hardwicke was the start of a dismal run for Hurricane Lane. On his first start since his close third in the 2021 Arc, he was a well-beaten odds-on favourite behind Broome. After finishing eighth in the Grand Prix de Saint-Cloud a fortnight later, also at odds-on, he wasn't seen again last year, and there was further disappointment when he was last of seven in the John Porter Stakes at Newbury on his reappearance in April.

Appleby persevered, fitting Hurricane Lane with cheekpieces on the gallops and then in the Jockey Club Stakes, and finally he was rewarded with a six-length victory. A Racing Post Rating of 122 put the performance up there with Hurricane Lane's Classic wins and only 3lb below his 2021 peak. Jockey William Buick said: "This is the Hurricane Lane we know."

Easy ground might be key to seeing that same Hurricane Lane at Royal Ascot. His five RPRs in the 120s have come on going no faster than good and it is highly unlikely he will run again on good to firm. That was the description for last year's Hardwicke and he recorded an RPR of 114.

In the right conditions, better will be expected this year.

## STAR RATING
★ ★ ★

Hurricane Lane bounces back to winning form at Newmarket in May

# Champion quality

BAY BRIDGE was a beaten odds-on favourite in last year's Prince of Wales's Stakes but returns to the royal meeting with enhanced credentials after winning the Champion Stakes over course and distance in October.

The Sir Michael Stoute-trained five-year-old gained a first top-level victory when defeating Adayar, who is likely to reoppose, by half a length in a race that saw Baaeed suffer a first defeat on his 11th and final start.

Bay Bridge is the one to beat on that form and on reflection his length second to State Of Rest in last year's Prince of Wales's can be marked up.

Stoute admitted "the race didn't pan out brilliantly" for Bay Bridge, with the lack of early pace against him, while it was the first time he had encountered good to firm ground – and he was a beaten favourite on the same going description in the Eclipse at Sandown on his next start.

However, for a first attempt at the top level, Bay Bridge's Prince of Wales's effort was full of promise and he confirmed that impression on Champions Day.

Those two runs suggest he is well suited by Ascot and Stoute is fond of this Group 1, winning with Hard Fought in 1981, Stagecraft a decade later, and more recently Poet's Word (2018) and Crystal Ocean (2019).

While there are few chinks in Bay Bridge's armour, underfoot conditions seem quite key. It was felt the very soft ground at Longchamp was against him on his return when third in a high-quality Prix Ganay in April, and his only other start on soft ground was a debut third at Yarmouth in 2020.

Following his return, joint-owner James Wigan said: "I think this ground just found him out a bit. Although he goes on the ground, it just made it that bit more difficult to get home. Ryan [Moore] said he thought he was going to pick them up, but it was his first start of the year and he probably needed it."

Bay Bridge has a 0-2 record on soft or very soft and good to firm but otherwise excels on ground between those extremes. He will have every chance of going one better than last year if conditions are in his favour on day two.

## STAR RATING
★★★★

Bay Bridge (Antonello Marcasciano) after exercising on Side Hill Canter in Newmarket and (right) winning on Champions Day

Owners: James Wigan & Ballylinch Stud
Trainer: Sir Michael Stoute

"He will have every chance of going one better than last year if conditions are in his favour on day two"

# Golden opportunity

SEEKING a stayer who performs best at Ascot and arrives at the top of his game? Look no further than Coltrane.

The Andrew Balding-trained six-year-old has run at the track three times in the past year, winning the Ascot Stakes at the royal meeting, finishing a head second to Trueshan in the Long Distance Cup and landing the Sagaro Stakes on his return this campaign.

As a stayer who had more than a year off the track following his three-year-old campaign due to injury, Coltrane is making up for lost time. His last two efforts were his best on Racing Post Ratings and right-handed, galloping Ascot clearly suits him particularly well.

In beating Wise Eagle, El Habeeb and regular rival Trueshan in the Sagaro, Coltrane has the edge over some of his likely opponents but the Gold Cup will require more. His rider Oisin Murphy believes Coltrane can find it.

"I was so impressed with that," he said after the Sagaro. "He relaxed great, the pace was slow but he took off when we got racing and he's in the form of his life. I'd hope he'd improve from that."

Does Coltrane have the required class and ability to win a Group 1? That is a fair question given his age, but he has had only one attempt.

Coltrane ran with great credit when fourth in the Goodwood Cup last year – a contest described by Racing Post analyst Mark Brown as "up there as one of the best staying races in recent times". He was beaten just under five lengths by Kyprios, with Stradivarius and Trueshan filling the places. The first two are not around now and Trueshan has shown signs of regression in two starts this term.

This year's Gold Cup will not be a race for the ages in terms of quality and the door has opened for Coltrane, a six-time winner and three-time runner-up from 12 turf starts. While unproven on soft ground, some of his best form has been with some ease underfoot and he has no problem with a sounder surface.

In what appears a particularly open running, this late bloomer is one to keep on side. This might just be his time.

## STAR RATING
★★★★

Coltrane lands
the Sagaro
Stakes at Ascot
(main and inset)

# Life in the fast lane

SAKHEER was so blindingly quick over six furlongs as a juvenile that many saw sprinting as his likely metier this year. The Commonwealth Cup, introduced in 2015 to cater for exactly that type of three-year-old, looked an ideal target.

In the spring there was the temptation to stretch him to a mile in the 2,000 Guineas, and his brilliance made it well worth the try, but seventh place at Newmarket brought the conversation back to the Commonwealth Cup. The arguments in favour of a sprinting campaign remained strong.

With a high cruising speed, tactical pace, another change of gear and a strong finish, Sakheer has long looked tailor-made for Ascot's stiff six furlongs. Even more so if mid-June brings fast ground, rather than the soft that blunted his speed and tested his stamina to the hilt in the Guineas.

There was a buzz around Sakheer from the moment he topped the Arqana breeze-up sale at €550,000 last May and it was a surprise to Roger Varian when he was beaten on his debut at Windsor three months later. He was quick to set the record straight, scooting six lengths clear in a Haydock novice and then stamping his authority on the Group 2 Mill Reef Stakes at Newbury with a three-and-a-half-length success.

An unsuccessful crack at the Guineas followed by a drop back in trip for the Commonwealth Cup is already a well-worn path, with three of the eight sprint winners having been well beaten in their Classic attempt. Last year Perfect Power was seventh at Newmarket before landing the Commonwealth Cup, precisely the turnaround that Sakheer would be attempting.

There are other informative similarities. Perfect Power was a dual Group 1 winner at two but his Racing Post Rating of 115 was exactly the same as Sakheer's, which puts Varian's challenger very much in the right ballpark. The highest juvenile RPR attained by a Commonwealth Cup winner is 117 (Caravaggio in 2017 and Advertise in 2018) and only three of the eight runnings have seen the winner run into the 120s.

There was every indication in the spring that Sakheer had trained on, with jockey David Egan describing him as "physically stronger" after his first gallop on him as a three-year-old. The Guineas may have been a disappointing start, but recent history shows there's plenty of time for Sakheer to reveal the true depth of his talent.

## STAR RATING
★★★★

Sakheer working on the Rowley Mile before his run in the 2,000 Guineas and (below) running away with last year's Mill Reef Stakes

# Supremely talented

LAST year's Derby hero Desert Crown would arguably be the most fascinating runner across the five days if he contests the Prince of Wales's Stakes.

Despite being one of the most high-profile and exciting horses in training, there are many unknowns about Desert Crown. What is his best trip? What are his ideal conditions? And, most importantly, just how good is he?

What we do know from his Classic success – when justifying 5-2 favouritism at Epsom last June – is that he's supremely talented. Desert Crown, who is also entered in the Hardwicke, recorded the joint-second-highest Racing Post Rating of 125 in the Derby in the past decade, a figure bettered only by Golden Horn's 127 in 2015.

He was eased a few strides from the winning post by Richard Kingscote – such luxuries are rarely taken in Classics – and Racing Post analyst Mark Brown felt he could be called the winner three furlongs out. "He's a top-class three-year-old who looks set to have a say in all the major middle-distance prizes this year," Brown wrote. "There'll be races such as the Eclipse, King George

and Irish Champion Stakes to consider before the Arc."

Unfortunately, we never saw Desert Crown in any of those races. A foot injury ruled him out of a crack at the King George in July and the International at York came too soon the following month.

The Champion Stakes and Prix de l'Arc de Triomphe were mentioned as possible end-of-season targets but connections decided to take a patient approach and focus on his four-year-old campaign.

Nonetheless, there are some notable pointers to Desert Crown's class from his two wins prior to last year's Derby. His back-end juvenile debut success in a 1m½f maiden at Nottingham

earned an RPR of 94, 4lb higher than three-time top-level scorers Space Blues and Mishriff, winners of the same race in 2018 and 2019.

Desert Crown's Dante win even correlated with his Derby success as, once again, it was only Golden Horn who had bettered his winning RPR in the previous ten years.

Golden Horn added the Eclipse, Irish Champion and Arc to his incredible CV before bowing out at the end of his three-year-old campaign. Desert Crown may be another year on but he might just be able to do something similar. Now that is exciting.

## STAR RATING
★★★★★

Owner: Saeed Suhail
Trainer: Sir Michael Stoute

Desert Crown at Sir Michael Stoute's Freemason Lodge base and (below) winning last year's Derby

# Meehan's new hotshot

BRIAN MEEHAN'S last top-level success came with Most Improved in the St James's Palace Stakes in 2012 and some interesting parallels can be drawn with his leading contender Isaac Shelby.

Most Improved, like Isaac Shelby, had three starts at two and showed a high level of form, with his sole start at three prior to Royal Ascot coming in the French Derby.

Kieren Fallon's mount was luckless at Chantilly, having been denied a clear run on several occasions, but he gained quick compensation at the royal meeting just over two weeks later when beating 2,000 Guineas third Hermival by three-quarters of a length.

While Isaac Shelby returned in April with a three-length win in the Greenham, his pre-Ascot outing similarly came in a French Classic when a

short-neck second to Marhaba Ya Sanafi in the French 2,000 Guineas at Longchamp.

Despite going very close to a first top-level success, Isaac Shelby recorded just a 1lb higher Racing Post Rating than when winning the Greenham, with Meehan feeling the lack of a strong gallop went against his talented colt.

"I'm a little frustrated with the pace," said Meehan. "In the middle third of the race they seemed to go a little steady for him. He's run a lovely race and there's more to come. I think he's a better horse than he showed today and the pace had something to do with it."

Isaac Shelby's RPR of 118 in the Greenham was higher than subsequent St James's Palace winner Barney Roy and last year's Commonwealth Cup scorer Perfect Power in the same race, so he certainly has the potential to rate higher, and his French Guineas RPR compares favourably with fellow leading contender Royal Scotsman – albeit 2lb shy of Chaldean.

Versatility is a key attribute for Isaac Shelby, whose sire Night Of Thunder won the 2,000 Guineas before finishing second to Kingman in the St James's Palace.

Isaac Shelby's three-year-old form is on soft and very soft ground, while his sole triple-figure RPR at two was recorded when winning the Group 2 Superlative Stakes on good to firm at Newmarket. He is equally adept going left- or right-handed.

He has run one bad race when trailing in last of seven behind Chaldean and Royal Scotsman in the Dewhurst Stakes last year, but his subsequent exploits proved it was not his true running.

It is 11 years since Most Improved's Royal Ascot heroics. Can Meehan repeat the trick? Isaac Shelby's profile suggests it could be possible.

## STAR RATING
★★★

Isaac Shelby records a comprehensive victory in the Greenham Stakes

# CV of a top stayer

FOUR-YEAR-OLDS have been much the most successful age group in the Gold Cup recently, winning seven of the last ten runnings, and Eldar Eldarov has the right credentials to extend that record.

Taking into account that Stradivarius had two of the three older successes in compiling his hat-trick after first striking at four, the younger age group has been the place to look for a new staying force.

At three Eldar Eldarov won both the Queen's Vase and St Leger – two of the key milestones for a potential Gold Cup winner. Of the seven four-year-olds to win the Gold Cup in the past decade, four had competed in at least one of those races the previous season – and two more would have done but for unfavourable circumstances (ground and a stalls problem).

Three of the seven had won one of those key races. Like Eldar Eldarov, the 2014 Gold Cup winner Leading Light had doubled up in the Queen's Vase and St Leger the previous year.

"An out-and-out Cup horse" was how Roger Varian described Eldar Eldarov in his Racing Post Stable Tour in the spring, identifying the Yorkshire Cup as the first stop on the road to Royal Ascot. Eldar Eldarov duly turned up there and, while he was beaten half a length by surprise winner Giavellotto, second place was a more than satisfactory start. With last year's Hardwicke Stakes winner Broome a length back in third, the form looked solid.

"He ran like he was the best in the field," Varian said. "He gave the winner 5lb and Broome 2lb. It was a really good run and you'd think the Gold Cup would suit him."

A niggling doubt is raised by Eldar Eldarov's poor run in the Long Distance Cup last October on his first attempt at two miles. He was seventh of eight, beaten 14 lengths by Trueshan on good to soft, and Varian was at a loss to explain that disappointment. "I'm not sure what happened," he said. "Maybe it was the ground."

The St Leger was won on good to soft, though probably not as testing as Ascot's turf deeper into the autumn, while it was good to firm for the Queen's Vase and again for the Yorkshire Cup.

That suggests a quicker surface will be in Eldar Eldarov's favour, but still he has to prove he stays two miles – let alone the two and a half of the Gold Cup.

Varian is confident . . . and there's only one way to find out.

## STAR RATING
★★★★

> **"He ran like he was the best in the field. He gave the winner 5lb and Broome 2lb. It was a really good run and you'd think the Gold Cup would suit him"**

# Tahiyra

Owner: HH The Aga Khan
Trainer: Dermot Weld

# Quicker surface expected to suit

DESPITE defeat on her return in the 1,000 Guineas, Tahiyra has strong claims as the class act among the potential runners in the Coronation Stakes.

The Aga Khan's filly ran to a Racing Post Rating of 116 when winning the Moyglare Stud Stakes on her second and final start at two – the same peak juvenile figure recorded by Inspiral, last year's Coronation winner, in the Fillies' Mile.

That rating is comfortably the highest recorded by the past ten Coronation winners at two, with Cheveley Park scorer Alcohol Free and Rizeena, who was similarly successful in the Moyglare, next best with RPRs of 113.

Tahiyra improved on her Moyglare RPR by 1lb when beaten half a length in the Newmarket Classic in May. On that form, she is closely matched with the winner Mawj, but it doesn't tell the whole story.

Mawj arrived at the Rowley Mile with the benefit of two winter runs at Meydan, whereas Dermot Weld was at pains prior to the race to inform punters he would have liked "a little more time" to prepare his star filly.

Weld reiterated his view after the race and took great encouragement from Tahiyra's fine effort. He said: "She's run a super race. She's very talented and has a lot of speed. It was just that her speed was nullified slightly by the soft ground. We were a bit in the dark about the ground as she has a lot of pace. We were about two weeks behind with her."

Tahiyra is unraced on ground quicker than good to yielding but, judging by Weld's post-race comments, a sounder surface would be more help than hindrance. She has standout credentials.

## STAR RATING
★★★★★

# Lezoo

Owners: Marc Chan & Andrew Rosen
Trainer: Ralph Beckett

THREE of the eight Commonwealth Cup winners failed to stay a mile in the 2,000 Guineas or French equivalent on their previous start and the drop back in trip from a Classic is the key angle for Lezoo backers.

Last year's Cheveley Park winner raced exclusively in sprints at two and stepped up in distance by two furlongs in the 1,000 Guineas. The combination of the extra trip and soft ground, having never raced in conditions easier than good, proved her undoing but punters should consider putting a line through her eighth-place finish.

Muhaarar, the inaugural Commonwealth Cup winner in 2015, finished eighth in the French 2,000 Guineas prior to Ascot, while Advertise was beaten out of sight at Newmarket before his royal success in 2019. Last year's winner Perfect Power arrived off the back of finishing seventh in the first Classic of the season.

This talented filly had beaten 1,000 Guineas heroine Mawj and leading Classic fancy Meditate when winning at the top level at Newmarket on her final start last year, recording a Racing Post Rating just 1lb shy of subsequent Coronation winner Alcohol Free's 2020 mark.

# Commonwealth history a factor

After that success, her trainer Ralph Beckett said: "She's just very, very good. We haven't had one as good as this at this stage. She doesn't show up at home really but has got better and better with racing."

Lezoo, the likely mount of Frankie Dettori at his final royal meeting, brings course-and-distance winning form, having landed the Princess Margaret Stakes last July, and should not be dismissed lightly.

If the ground is on the quicker side, a return to her best could be forthcoming in a race won by two fillies – Quiet Reflection and Campanelle – in its short history.

## STAR RATING
★★★

139

# Waiting in the wings

INSPIRAL is the star older filly heading to Royal Ascot but this stablemate looks capable of a leading role and it is still possible she could play a part in Royal Ascot's opening act.

Laurel was the stand-in for Inspiral in the Group 1 Lockinge Stakes and, while it would be unfair to say she fluffed her lines entirely, it wasn't the performance many had hoped to see. Sent off the 100-30 second favourite, she trailed home tenth behind Modern Games, who just headed her in the betting but proved far superior in the race.

The upshot was that Modern Games took over as favourite for the Queen Anne Stakes, the coveted first race of the royal meeting. Inspiral, heading straight there after not being quite ready for the Lockinge, was next in the market but Laurel did not drift out of the picture – and that's because there were mitigating circumstances for her Lockinge disappointment.

She sat a few lengths off Mutasaabeq on the far side of the field but found herself without cover and ultimately a little isolated when the main action unfolded towards the stands' side. The last 11 British-trained

winners of the Queen Anne ran in the Lockinge and several were well beaten, so all is not lost yet.

Having said that, Laurel has something to find on Racing Post Ratings. Her best is the 114 she recorded when a close second to Fonteyn in the Sun Chariot Stakes last autumn on her first attempt in a Group 1. By comparison, Inspiral has an RPR of 123 from her dominant Coronation Stakes

victory at last year's royal meeting.

If Inspiral returns in top shape, Laurel could be moved to Wednesday's Group 2 Duke of Cambridge Stakes, also over the straight mile. Arguably that might be more her standard for now and she would have a leading chance, but there is certainly top-level potential too.

## STAR RATING
★★★

# Emily Dickinson

Owners: Mrs John Magnier/Michael Tabor/Derrick Smith/Westerberg; Trainer: Aidan O'Brien

# A new hope for O'Brien

IN THE absence of star stayer Kyprios, Aidan O'Brien has been searching for his Gold Cup challenger. On the same day in mid-May, he tried Broome in the Yorkshire Cup and Emily Dickinson in the Saval Beg Stakes, and both came up short. But it could be a different story in mid-June.

Punters will certainly have faith in O'Brien, the master trainer of stayers. He proved that again last year when Kyprios gave him an eighth Gold Cup and went on to dominate the staying scene. A repeat scenario seemed on the cards until O'Brien revealed in March that infection in a joint would keep Kyprios on the sidelines.

Emily Dickinson looked the obvious replacement, having ended last year with a convincing victory in the Group 3 Loughbrown Stakes at the Curragh when upped to two miles. She "grew a leg" that day, in O'Brien's words, and he pointed her down the Gold Cup road.

Her season started well with a five-length victory in the Vintage Crop Stakes at Navan but then she was only sixth in the Saval Beg, the second main Irish stepping stone to the Gold Cup. Broome had been third at York a few hours earlier and it was a double setback, but

far from a mortal blow to O'Brien's hopes.

Certainly in the case of Emily Dickinson, always viewed as the more likely of the pair to relish the two and a half miles of the Gold Cup, there are reasons to expect a turnaround. The muddling pace in the 1m6f Saval Beg was against her and she will be better when held on to for longer with more cut in the ground over a longer trip. She could get all those things at Royal Ascot.

In an open Gold Cup, she still has plenty to recommend her.

## STAR RATING
★★★★

# Has Trail gone cold?

CLASSIC winner Native Trail has the ability to go well in the Queen Anne Stakes but his reappearance at Newmarket's Guineas meeting provided more questions than answers.

After a three-year-old campaign that included Irish 2,000 Guineas victory, second place in the 2,000 Guineas at Newmarket and a close third in the Eclipse, there was plenty of hope that Native Trail could blossom further this term.

The market suggested he was going to stamp his authority on his four rivals in the bet365 Mile at Newmarket but the 8-11 favourite was fairly underwhelming, making no impression on all-the-way winner Mutasaabeq, who had 9lb to find with Native Trail at the weights.

Mutasaabeq benefited from having the run of the race, and at one point it looked like Native Trail would do well to hold on to second, a feat he just managed with a short head to spare over Light Infantry.

Andrew Sheret analysed the Group 2 for the Racing Post and wrote: "It's too soon to suggest Native Trail's best days are behind him but he couldn't be supported with confidence in a Group 1 next time."

Taking the form at face value, Native Trail will be unlikely to trouble the Queen Anne principals. Charlie Appleby, however, has not lost faith in the talented colt, whose other Group 1 successes came at two in the National and Dewhurst Stakes.

Appleby said: "William

[Buick] was pleased and said Native Trail was just a bit rusty. You could see from the gate he was just having to chivvy him along a little bit. He said he'll sharpen up no end on that but that the most important thing was that he wanted it.

"He nursed him across the line given how long he has been off. Not all is lost there at all."

Successful on six of his first seven starts, Native Trail has now been beaten on his last three outings and doubts remain over whether he can bounce back to his best.

A return to his peak three-year-old form would put him in the mix but that will require a 10lb improved effort on Racing Post Ratings

from his Newmarket return to his first visit to Ascot.

That has to be a concern and so does any ease in the ground, with Native Trail unraced on easier than good to yielding.

## STAR RATING
★★★

Native Trail: question marks over his recent form

# A question of distance

THERE was a statement of intent from owner-breeders Cheveley Park Stud after Sacred strode clear for an impressive winning return in Group 3 company on the all-weather at Lingfield in May.

Max McLoughlin, management assistant to Cheveley Park, said: "We've kept her in training to try to win a Group 1 because we think she's that good. She's got two entries at Ascot; the problem is seven furlongs is her best trip."

Sacred's preference for seven furlongs is an undeniable issue when it comes to the royal meeting. There is no race for her over that intermediate trip and the options are to go up to a mile in the Duke of Cambridge Stakes, a Group 2, or down to the Queen Elizabeth II Jubilee Stakes over six furlongs. Last year she ran in the sprint Group 1 and was a creditable fifth, beaten just a length in a bunch finish.

Ryan Moore, who is 2-2 on Sacred and was aboard for her most recent success, also saw the problem for connections.

"She's a seven-furlong filly and it's hard to find those Group 1 races for her," he said.

In last year's Platinum Jubilee, Sacred was a 15-2 shot on her first start of the season and came under pressure before the two-furlong pole. She responded admirably to Tom Marquand's urgings and got close, giving the impression

an extra furlong would have very much suited.

Connections took the same view as she has raced over seven furlongs in five starts since, winning the Dubai Duty Free Cup at Newbury in September, and more often than not done her best work late. There has been little to suggest a drop back in trip would favour her.

Sacred had enough speed at two to finish a three-quarter-length runner-up to Campanelle over the minimum trip in the Queen Mary Stakes – her only other start at Ascot – so she goes well at the course.

Connections feel significant ease in the ground does not suit Sacred, although she ran well on her sole start on good to soft when runner-up in the Lowther Stakes as a juvenile.

She tends to go particularly well fresh, so while she proved her wellbeing at Lingfield, she is not certain to back that up in stronger company. The five-year-old has been beaten on her second start in each season.

There are enough reasons to take on Sacred in whichever race she contests. The elusive Group 1 may well be won this season but it seems more likely to come at her optimum trip.

## STAR RATING
★★★

# Beckett filly set for big battle

Haskoy: Gold Cup now on her agenda

### HASKOY
**Owner:** Juddmonte
**Trainer:** Ralph Beckett

Haskoy will carry plenty of potential into the Gold Cup, albeit with less in the way of experience, if she is allowed to take her chance by Ralph Beckett.

The trainer views the 2m4f showpiece as a somewhat unforgiving race but was more inclined to send Haskoy there after her reappearance win in the Group 3 Al Rayyan Stakes at Newbury on Lockinge day. The four-year-old battled well to score by a short head over Israr and make it three wins in just four starts since her belated debut in late July last year.

Her sole defeat came in a rough St Leger when she finished two lengths behind Eldar Eldarov in second but was demoted to fourth for causing interference. That is high-class form in terms of this year's stayers as Eldar Eldarov came out to be second in the Yorkshire Cup behind Giavellotto (originally fourth in the St Leger) and Emily Dickinson (fifth at Doncaster) is a leading Gold Cup hope for Aidan O'Brien.

Haskoy halved in price to 8-1 for the Gold Cup after her Newbury win, which again emphasised her appetite for a fight despite

Shaquille: Group 1 hope for Julie Camacho

her inexperience. That could be a key factor.

"The Gold Cup is a big ask for any horse," Beckett said. "It's more like a war than a horserace. It's tough for all of them, and some never come back from it, but I'm more inclined to do it now she's won a Group race."

## SHAQUILLE

**Owners: Hughes, Rawlings, O'Shaughnessy**
**Trainer: Julie Camacho**

This flying three-year-old may well be one of the bigger chances for a smaller yard if he takes up his entry in the Group 1 Commonwealth Cup.

That looked more likely after an impressive win in the Listed Carnarvon Stakes at Newbury, which has become an important marker for the Royal Ascot contest. It was another step up for Shaquille after a decisive handicap victory at Newmarket on his reappearance a fortnight earlier.

Having dwelt at the start at Newmarket, he took a keen

hold before powering home by two and three-quarter lengths. He was equally on top at Newbury, making all to score by two lengths and take his record to five wins out of six.

Shaquille can be tricky to handle on raceday and the key will be keeping a lid on his temperament but not on his speed.

"He wants to be fast and I think we should let him be quick. He can motor on," was James Doyle's view from the saddle at Newbury.

"He must have some engine to do what he did at Newmarket," said trainer Julie Camacho, who might just find that Shaquille powers her to a first top-level success.

## MY PROSPERO

**Owner: Sunderland Holding Inc**
**Trainer: William Haggas**

With high-class Group 1 form at Ascot, My Prospero should pose a big threat whichever entry he takes up at the royal meeting. After

his reappearance fourth in the Lockinge over a mile, it seems more likely that he will step back up in trip to contest the Prince of Wales's Stakes.

Trying him back at a mile on his first run as a four-year-old seemed a reasonable call – after all, he was beaten only narrowly in third behind Coroebus in last year's St James's Palace Stakes - but his Lockinge fourth behind Modern Games seemed to confirm he would prove best at a mile and a quarter.

That was the trip where he scored a Group 2 success in France last summer before concluding his season with a career-best performance in third behind Bay Bridge and Adayar in the Champion Stakes. That was a second top-level loss at Ascot by less than a length and merited a Racing Post Rating of 124, with the promise of better to come this year.

Even if he stands still, his 2022 form makes him a big player for the Prince of Wales's.

# 'He's a Coventry horse'

## RIVER TIBER

When Democracy made a winning start for Aidan O'Brien in mid-April, there were whispers at the Curragh that stablemate River Tiber – withdrawn on account of the heavy ground – was the better prospect. Less than a week later, this Wootton Bassett colt appeared to prove the point with a stunning Navan debut under Ryan Moore that made him the first juvenile to break three figures on Racing Post Ratings this season.

The ground was soft for the 5½f contest but that proved no issue for River Tiber, who powered up the hill to win easily by ten lengths. The opposition may not have been that strong – the runner-up and fourth were both well beaten next time – but he was seriously impressive.

His debut RPR of 104 marked him out as a strong Coventry Stakes candidate. In comparison, the highest pre-race RPR for a Coventry winner in the past decade was 106 for O'Brien's Caravaggio in 2016, but that came on his second start and he rated nearly a stone lower on his debut at 94.

River Tiber followed up in the 5f Coolmore Stud Calyx Race on good ground at Naas and, while it wasn't so visually impressive, O'Brien was satisfied enough with a two-and-a-half-length victory over Tourist, who had run Ballydoyle's Johannes Brahms close on his debut.

"I'm very happy we ran him," O'Brien said. "He's not done anything to take him off the bridle at home and at Navan he won very easily, so he probably didn't know a lot. I thought he might not even come off the bridle today, but the runner-up is obviously a good horse and took him off it."

As for his Royal Ascot prospects, the trainer added: "We thought he'd be a Coventry horse. Ryan felt the quicker ground was no problem to him and he won't get ground any quicker than that at Ascot."

## PORTA FORTUNA

River Tiber was a talking point after his second run at Naas but this Donnacha O'Brien-trained daughter of Caravaggio was also on many lips after her Group 3 success in the 6f Fillies Sprint, which likewise took her to a 2-2 record and put her on course for Royal Ascot.

Having scored by a neck over 5f at the Curragh on her debut, she prevailed by the same margin up in class and distance. Navassa Island was eating into her lead all the way to the line but Porta Fortuna kept on strongly with another brave effort.

"We thought she was a nice filly, but obviously you never expect to win a Group race with a filly that's had one run," O'Brien said on Racing TV. "There's probably a good chance she'll go to Ascot. If she does it will probably be for the Albany. She looked to get a stiff six furlongs here well. She handles all kinds of ground, so I wouldn't be worried either way."

## NO NAY METS

This year saw the launch of US automatic qualifiers for Royal Ascot, with the winners of two juvenile five-furlong turf races at Gulfstream Park on May 13 given automatic entry into one of the six two-year-old races at the royal meeting along with $25,000 towards equine travel costs.

If the aim was to extend Ascot's appeal beyond regular visitor Wesley Ward, there was an immediate reward as trainer George Weaver took both races and pointed the winners towards the big meeting.

In the first of them, the Royal Palm Juvenile, victory went to debutant No Nay Mets, who made all to score by three and a half lengths. Ward's Holding The Line was odds-on favourite but finished seventh.

The Coolmore-bred winner is a son of No Nay Never, who was one of Ward's early Royal Ascot winners in the 2013 Norfolk Stakes. Described by Weaver as "a pretty nifty colt", No Nay Mets could well go for the same five-furlong contest.

## CRIMSON ADVOCATE

Having won the first US automatic qualifier, George Weaver quickly added the second when Crimson Advocate took the Royal Palm Juvenile Fillies on the same Gulfstream Park card. It was a near carbon copy of the first race as Weaver's daughter of Nyquist made all and won by the identical margin of three and a half lengths, except that she was more than a second quicker than No Nay Mets in an impressive 56.25 seconds.

Crimson Advocate did have the benefit of previous experience over her stablemate, however, and her greenness when third on her debut prompted Weaver to fit blinkers for the Ascot qualifier. The headgear did the trick as the filly was much more polished in defeating Ocean Mermaid, the Wesley Ward-trained odds-on favourite. The first two are set to renew rivalry at Royal Ascot, quite possibly in the Queen Mary.

Weaver has tried the royal meeting before, when Cyclogenisis finished down the field in the inaugural Commonwealth Cup, but this is set to be his first attempt with juveniles.

"I always said after I went to Ascot the first time it would be nice to go back with someone who has a chance of winning and both of these horses look like they do," he said. "They have that early speed. I need to look at the menu before picking out a race, although I'd like to keep both of them at five-eighths [five furlongs] if we can."

## RELIEF RALLY

The double green colours of Simon Munir and Isaac Souede, so familiar in the big jumps races, could get a prominent showing at Royal Ascot with this William Haggas-trained filly.

The daughter of Kodiac took a Windsor novice on soft ground in late April and followed up three weeks later in a fillies' conditions race at Salisbury, both times over 5f and with a winning distance of around two lengths. The second victory was given a Racing Post Rating of 93, putting her firmly in the reckoning for Royal Ascot.

Anthony Bromley, the owners' racing manager, said: "She's a little pocket rocket and it's really exciting. She's not the biggest but she looks all speed."

That points to the Queen Mary, where Relief Rally would have to take on at least one US speedball. She might just be up to beating them at their own game.

## JABAARA

This daughter of Exceed And Excel was a first juvenile winner of the season for Roger Varian and the choice of launchpad was also noteworthy. The 6f fillies' novice she won at Newmarket on May 20 was landed by subsequent 1,000 Guineas winners Cachet and Mawj in the previous two years and Jabaara will take the same route as that pair and head next for the Albany Stakes at Royal Ascot.

Neither of them won the Albany, but Varian's Daahyeh did in 2019 after a successful debut in the Newmarket race and he anticipates another bold showing with Jabaara, who opened her account by three-quarters of a length under David Egan.

Varian said: "This filly has always looked smart at home. She was a touch green in the race and David had to take her off heels and start his run again, but she pricked her ears passing the line. We've been lucky enough to win the Albany twice before and we think this filly is up there."

# 'Well above average'

## AMERICAN RASCAL

US trainer Wesley Ward's strong team of juveniles is headed by this Norfolk Stakes-bound colt, who is replete with Royal Ascot connections. The son of Curlin is the first foal out of the Ward-trained Lady Aurelia, who won the Queen Mary Stakes as a juvenile in 2016 and returned the following year to take the King's Stand Stakes.

Her combined winning distance in those two races was ten lengths and there was something of her explosive ability in American Rascal's runaway debut win in a maiden special weight at Keeneland in April. He scorched home by ten and a quarter lengths, almost seven years to the day since Lady Aurelia won her first race in similarly dominant fashion at the Kentucky track.

Ward, who often gives his Royal Ascot juveniles a single run over Keeneland's four and a half furlongs, said: "American Rascal has come out of his first race in super shape. The team really liked him and it was exciting to see him produce a performance like that."

What comes next could be even more exciting.

## FANDOM

Seven of Wesley Ward's eight juvenile winners at Royal Ascot debuted over Keeneland's four and a half furlongs on dirt, and none had run beyond five, so Fandom has the unusual distinction of having started his career on turf at Keeneland over five and a half furlongs.

The Showcasing colt looked a typical Ward early two-year-old in the race, though, with a fast start and dominant all-the-way win by six and three-quarter lengths. It was a thoroughly professional performance and the speed he showed far from precludes a drop back to five furlongs for the Norfolk or Windsor Castle Stakes.

This Ward juvenile is British-bred and was bought at last year's Tattersalls October Yearling Sale, fetching 170,000gns for Andrew Black's Chasemore Farm.

His dam's sire Pivotal won the King's Stand Stakes and her half-sister Lezoo landed last year's Cheveley Park Stakes at Newmarket, which adds to his credentials for a strong showing back on British soil.

## MAXIMUM IMPACT

Newmarket trainer Alice Haynes sent out her first Ascot winner when Maximum Impact took the five-furlong juvenile contest on trials day in early May and now has the royal meeting in her sights.

The son of Havana Grey recorded a Rating Post Rating of 97 (one of the best in the early season) as he battled to victory by two and a quarter lengths, suggesting a step up to six furlongs for the Coventry might be in order.

That confirmed the promise of his 12-length debut success at Leicester, although the form had been questionable as the ground was heavy and the race was started by flag. Good ground at Ascot brought an improved performance from the Amo Racing youngster, who could go for the Norfolk if Haynes opts to stay at the minimum trip.

"Well above average" was the verdict from Haynes, one of the rising young trainers, and jockey Kevin Stott added: "When he first won it wasn't really much of a race. I think he'll come on a lot more for the Ascot run than his first run. I really liked the way he put his head down."

## HIS MAJESTY

This Aidan O'Brien-trained colt, foaled on January 5, 2021, may well be the oldest juvenile at this year's Royal Ascot and a look at the key pointers on pages 30-33 will tell you how significant that could be. It is far from the only positive factor, however, as the son of No Nay Never was quick to show his talent on the track with a Listed success at the Curragh first time out.

The field was weakened by the withdrawals of previous winners Bucanero Fuerte and Noche Magica but His Majesty still had to cope with soft ground and stablemate Unquestionable, who was favourite, and did it well to take the five-furlong contest by three-quarters of a length.

A Racing Post Rating of 96 confirmed his quality and O'Brien said: "He has loads of speed and is big and mature. He'll have no problem with six furlongs."

That seemed an obvious step after it took His Majesty a while to get going over the minimum trip and Ascot's stiff six should pose no problem. No Nay Never has already sired a Coventry Stakes winner for O'Brien in Arizona and this candidate has strong claims.

## DEVIOUS

This Starspangledbanner colt could be the one to put Donnacha O'Brien on the Royal Ascot trainers' scoreboard alongside father Aidan and brother Joseph. Described as a natural by his trainer, Devious scored a smooth two-length victory on his debut in a five-furlong Naas maiden with a smart Racing Post Rating of 94.

O'Brien went to Naas thinking Devious was a Coventry Stakes candidate but the colt showed so much speed that he was inclined to keep him at the minimum trip for the Norfolk Stakes instead.

"Devious shouldn't be that fast, being that big and strong, so I'd say he's a proper horse," O'Brien said. "We have nothing that can take him off the bridle at home. He's got so much boot that the nice ground helps him but he would get slower ground as well as he's big and powerful."

The younger O'Brien may well have to get past his father to land a Royal Ascot first, but in Devious he has a strong challenger.

## ON POINT

Godolphin trainer Charlie Appleby enjoyed great days at Royal Ascot with Blue Point and could be set for more success with this son of his Platinum Jubilee and dual King's Stand Stakes winner.

On Point was one of the quick starters for the first-season sire, recording a Racing Post Rating of 90 with a debut success in a five-furlong maiden at Newmarket on 1,000 Guineas day. The ground was soft and there were only three runners, resulting in no more than a steady pace, but On Point battled well to record a head victory over Richard Hannon's Mashadi.

As his stable's first two-year-old runner of the season, On Point put himself in the Royal Ascot picture and the Norfolk Stakes looks a likely destination. "We were very keen to have a Blue Point winner," Appleby said at Newmarket. "It's fantastic and what you love to see is that he's shown all the characteristics that his dad showed as a two-year-old, with showing up early and having natural speed."

66 We have nothing that can take him off the bridle at home. He's got so much boot that the nice ground helps him but he would get slower ground as well as he's big and powerful 99

# 'He could be very good'

## SOPRANO

George Boughey won last year's 1,000 Guineas for Highclere Thoroughbreds with Cachet and this looks another filly with good prospects for the team.

The 100,000gns yearling made a winning debut over 5f at Newmarket's Guineas meeting, scoring by a length and three-quarters to earn a Racing Post Rating of 91. That is a little higher than Cachet's debut mark before she finished fifth in the 2021 Albany Stakes at Royal Ascot. Boughey's Oscula was third in that fillies' Group 3, off a pre-race RPR of 90, which marks out Soprano's effort as a more than satisfactory debut.

Even more so considering Boughey's initial surprise that the big, rangy daughter of Starspangledbanner was forward enough to be working well in the spring. She did so well that she turned out to be his first juvenile winner of the season and well up to scratch for a crack at the Albany.

## MIDNIGHT AFFAIR

The Newmarket 5f fillies' maiden won by Soprano may well turn out to be strong form and runner-up

Midnight Affair is also one to note. If both turn up at Royal Ascot, neither will lack for supporters.

The Richard Fahey-trained Midnight Affair was 5-1 third favourite on that racecourse bow, with Soprano heading the market at 6-4, and perhaps that was a reflection of the fact that her stable's juveniles were generally in need of their first run.

The race certainly didn't go her way as she ran into trouble a furlong out and had to be switched to the outside. She picked up in eyecatching fashion but Soprano had first run and finished the job off strongly. The margin was a length and three-quarters but they are closely matched on Racing Post Ratings, with Midnight Affair just 1lb behind on 90.

## NOCHE MAGICA

Juvenile debuts don't come much better than Noche Magica's performance in a Cork maiden on April 8, especially considering Paddy Twomey's colt had to overcome some difficulty.

Clearly plenty was expected of this £230,000 purchase, who was strong in the betting market at 7-4 just

behind Ballydoyle newcomer Alabama, but a slow start put him on the back foot. He responded impressively to challenge on the bridle a furlong out and then kick on to win decisively by three and three-quarter lengths.

Runner-up Sturlasson was a yardstick to the early Irish juveniles, having previously been a length closer to Adrian Murray's promising Bucanero Fuerte, and Noche Magica was given a Racing Post Rating of 93.

More would have been learned if Noche Magica, Bucanero Fuerte and Sturlasson had competed as planned in the Curragh Listed event won by His Majesty on May 1, but they were all withdrawn for various reasons. The one given for Noche Magica was a stone bruise.

That could leave him short of experience but certainly not of talent on the evidence of his debut.

## GOT TO LOVE A GREY

Karl Burke's juveniles merit considerable respect at Royal Ascot and he has a number of good prospects this year, including the colts Cuban Slide, Valour And Swagger and Elite Status.

But the one to highlight is

the filly Got To Love A Grey, who will bid to give her trainer back-to-back wins in the Queen Mary after Dramatised's success last year. Following a six-length debut win at Nottingham, she took the Listed Marygate Fillies' Stakes at York, often a race to note, with stablemate Dorothy Lawrence in second.

Burke said he was surprised at the finishing order of his two fillies, although the betting had it right with Got To Love A Grey at 5-2 and Dorothy Lawrence 9-1.

The trainer said: "Dorothy Lawrence didn't quite see it out as well as Got To Love A Grey, who's so honest and such a lovely filly. Got To Love A Grey will definitely go to Ascot. You need to stay well there, so it probably makes sense to go for the Queen Mary."

Dorothy Lawrence may well join her on the trip to Royal Ascot, where Burke looks set to field a strong team.

## MON NA SLIEVE

This Kevin Ryan-trained colt was bought for 190,000gns at the Tattersalls Craven Breeze-Up Sale on April 18 with Royal Ascot in mind and almost exactly a month later he fuelled the dream with a smart debut success in a 5f novice at York.

He earned a Racing Post Rating of 93 with his victory by a length and three-quarters from Richard Hannon's Mashadi, who had previously finished second to Godolphin's On Point.

Having been readied for the breeze-up, Mon Na Slieve was pretty sharp and Ryan said he was quietly confident heading to York, where he tends to introduce his better juveniles. The son of Exceed And Excel made all, showing plenty of speed.

"He's all five furlongs but he relaxes," Ryan told Racing TV. "He could have been dropped in but he's so professional he was able to make it."

The Norfolk or Windsor Castle Stakes, both won by Ryan before, will be the aim.

## DAPPER VALLEY

Two years ago Berkshire Shadow won the 5f newcomers' race at Newbury's Greenham meeting and landed the Coventry Stakes on his next outing, making it a race worth noting.

That was certainly the case this year when Richard Hannon's Dapper Valley scored by two and a quarter lengths. The third and fourth both won next time, boosting the form.

Hannon's juveniles tend not to be fully wound up for their debuts, which made Dapper Valley's winning RPR of 93 on soft ground a notable achievement.

"I was worried about running him on the ground," Hannon admitted, "but he's always shown up a good bit at home and I loved the way he travelled. He could be a very good two-year-old."

Got To Love A Grey (6):
Queen Mary contender

# First-class travellers

INTERNATIONAL success was on the menu again at Royal Ascot last year – and what a mouthwatering treat it was.

Ten years on from the great Black Caviar, Australia's sprinting dominance was restored by Nature Strip's blistering triumph in the King's Stand Stakes. Not only was it one of the standout feats of last year's royal meeting, the four-and-a-half-length demolition ranked high among the best sprinting performances seen in Europe this century.

While it was the first victory for Australia at Royal Ascot since Black Caviar's hearts-in-mouths success in the then Diamond Jubilee Stakes in 2012, it was their seventh Group 1 sprint win since Choisir's ground-breaking double in 2003 and it seems to have reinvigorated the overseas challenge for the meeting's big prizes.

This year's international entries for the eight Group 1 races include stars from Australia, Hong Kong and the US – all racing jurisdictions that have achieved notable landmarks at Royal Ascot – alongside the usual array of Group 1 winners from Britain, Ireland and France.

The sprints are being targeted in a big way again by a strong Australian contingent. Flying filly Coolangatta will lead the way in the King's Stand on the opening day after securing her second Group 1 victory for joint-trainers Ciaron Maher and David Eustace in the Lightning Stakes at Flemington in February – significantly, that five-furlong dash was won by every one of Australia's Royal Ascot winners.

Artorius, beaten less than a length in third in last year's Platinum Jubilee Stakes, is being aimed at another attempt by Anthony and Sam Freedman and is set to be joined by The Astrologist for Leon and Troy Corstens, another father-and-son team.

The US challenge will be led again by Wesley Ward, who has had 12 Royal Ascot winners since 2009. His big sprint duo are Twilight Gleaming (King's Stand) and Love Reigns (Commonwealth Cup or King's Stand) and he will have his usual brigade of juvenile runners, spearheaded by American Rascal in the Norfolk Stakes. The Curlin colt is the first foal out of Ward's Queen Mary and King's Stand winner Lady Aurelia.

Exciting depth to the American squad is added by entries for Brad Cox's Breeders' Cup Turf Sprint heroine Caravel and the Kenny McPeek-trained Classic Causeway, who could be a rare US runner in the Prince of Wales's Stakes. Another to note in the Commonwealth Cup is the Jorge Delgado-trained New York Thunder.

Hong Kong, also noted for fast horses and with wins on the board in the then Golden Jubilee and King's Stand, is set to have a first representative since 2016 in top-class sprinter Wellington. Richard Gibson's Group 1 Hong Kong Sprint winner holds entries in both of those big contests.

With such quality in the mix, the overseas raiders look set to bring plenty of excitement with them.

## WINNERS FROM OUTSIDE GB & IRE SINCE 2000

- France 23
- US 13
- Australia 7
- Hong Kong 2
- Germany 1
- Spain 1

Nature Strip's rider James McDonald greets
Chris Waller after last year's King's Stand

## WINNERS FROM OUTSIDE EUROPE SINCE 2000

| Year | Horse | Trainer | Country | Race |
|------|-------|---------|---------|------|
| 2003 | Choisir | Paul Perry | AUSTRALIA | King's Stand Stakes |
|      | Choisir | Paul Perry | AUSTRALIA | Golden Jubilee Stakes |
| 2005 | Cape Of Good Hope | David Oughton | HONG KONG | Golden Jubilee Stakes |
| 2006 | Takeover Target | Joe Janiak | AUSTRALIA | King's Stand Stakes |
| 2007 | Miss Andretti | Lee Freedman | AUSTRALIA | King's Stand Stakes |
| 2009 | Scenic Blast | Daniel Morton | AUSTRALIA | King's Stand Stakes |
|      | Strike The Tiger | Wesley Ward | USA | Windsor Castle Stakes |
|      | Jealous Again | Wesley Ward | USA | Queen Mary Stakes |
| 2012 | Little Bridge | Danny Shum | HONG KONG | King's Stand Stakes |
|      | Black Caviar | Peter Moody | AUSTRALIA | Diamond Jubilee Stakes |
| 2013 | No Nay Never | Wesley Ward | USA | Norfolk Stakes |
| 2014 | Hootenanny | Wesley Ward | USA | Windsor Castle Stakes |
| 2015 | Acapulco | Wesley Ward | USA | Queen Mary Stakes |
|      | Undrafted | Wesley Ward | USA | Diamond Jubilee Stakes |
| 2016 | Tepin | Mark Casse | USA | Queen Anne Stakes |
|      | Lady Aurelia | Wesley Ward | USA | Queen Mary Stakes |
| 2017 | Lady Aurelia | Wesley Ward | USA | King's Stand Stakes |
|      | Con Te Partiro | Wesley Ward | USA | Sandringham Handicap |
| 2018 | Shang Shang Shang | Wesley Ward | USA | Norfolk Stakes |
| 2020 | Campanelle | Wesley Ward | USA | Queen Mary Stakes |
| 2021 | Campanelle | Wesley Ward | USA | Commonwealth Cup |
| 2022 | Nature Strip | Chris Waller | AUSTRALIA | King's Stand Stakes |

## 202 RUNNERS FROM OUTSIDE EUROPE
## HAVE COMPETED AT ROYAL ASCOT SINCE 2003

# Lightning quick

STILL a three-year-old until August 1 in the southern hemisphere, Coolangatta has built a big reputation in a short time for joint-trainers Ciaron Maher and David Eustace.

After winning her first three starts at two, including the richly endowed Magic Millions Classic, Coolangatta tasted defeat for the first time when three lengths adrift of Fireburn in the 2022 Golden Slipper at a sodden Rosehill.

Her career record of five wins from eight starts also includes a soft-ground defeat in the Coolmore Stud Stakes last October – the daughter of Written Tycoon was withdrawn from the previous weekend's Manikato Stakes on similar going – and a wet June in Britain would certainly be a negative for her chances.

Focusing on the positives, Coolangatta will arrive off the back of victory in the Black Caviar Lightning Stakes, Australia's most important weight-for-age sprint over five furlongs.

The 2023 edition of the race was well named and, towed into the race by last season's King's Stand winner Nature Strip, she powered home up the pancake-flat straight at Flemington in closing furlong splits of 10.51, 10.52 and 11.35 seconds.

She was getting all the age and sex allowances but it was still a statement performance, as she became the first three-year-old filly to win the race since Regimental Gal in 2004.

In the context of taking on Europe's best, she looks a cut above, while her light race schedule means she could still be open to plenty of improvement.

Maher and Eustace haven't entered her in the six-furlong Queen Elizabeth II Jubilee Stakes but her ability to perform over the slightly longer trip around a bend, combined with a killer

mid-race kick, means Coolangatta shouldn't be considered as potentially vulnerable late in the race.

It will more likely be a question of whether any of her challengers can live with her between the three-furlong marker and the one pole.

Jamie Kah partnered Coolangatta to Group 1 victories in both the Lightning and the Moir Stakes but is on the long road to recovery after being hospitalised with severe concussion following a fall in March.

James McDonald knows the filly well after riding her in all four starts at two and will attempt to go back to back in the King's Stand after last year's win on Nature Strip.

Australia's speedballs dominated the King's Stand between Choisir in 2003 and Scenic Blast in 2009, with all four of their winners completing the Lightning-Ascot double.

After Nature Strip regained that thread in 2022, Australian fans and professionals will be expecting a return to 'business as usual', with Coolangatta arguably the visiting team's most credentialed contender.

## STAR RATING
★★★★★

Coolangatta (right): Lightning winner has first-class credentials

# Breeders' Cup star on a roll

Caravel and Tyler Gaffalione after their
Turf Sprint win for trainer Brad Cox (inset)

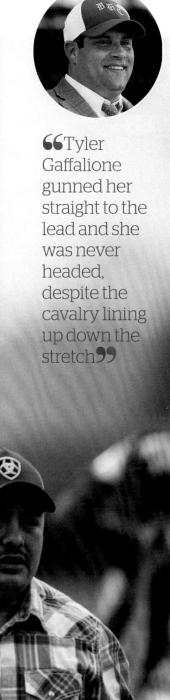

**"Tyler Gaffalione gunned her straight to the lead and she was never headed, despite the cavalry lining up down the stretch"**

EVEN at the very top level there is a tendency for sprinters to take turns in beating one another. So there is much to admire in the streak that Qatar Racing's Caravel has compiled over the past nine months, the string of 1s next to her name proof that, despite turning six years old, the daughter of Mizzen Mast is in the form of her life.

A comfortable Grade 3 success against her own sex in Keeneland's Franklin Stakes last October was deemed by bettors almost inconsequential when it came to the Breeders' Cup Turf Sprint over the same turning five and a half furlongs three weeks later, with Caravel sent off an unconsidered 43-1 shot.

Tyler Gaffalione gunned her straight to the lead – at the same moment favourite Golden Pal blew the start, much as he had in the 2022 King's Stand – and she was never headed, despite the cavalry lining up down the stretch.

What must have given Sheikh Fahad and trainer Brad Cox confidence to target Ascot was the fact that three of Britain's leading turf sprinters – Emaraaty Ana, Creative Force and Highfield Princess – all appeared to run their races in finishing second, third and fourth.

Keeneland was also where Cox chose to bring Caravel back in 2023 and she went wire-to-wire in the Grade 2 Shakertown Stakes, a race favoured by Wesley Ward for his older Ascot aspirants.

After keeping her on the go with eight starts in 2022, Cox wasn't about to take his foot off the accelerator and moved up the road to Churchill Downs, where Caravel landed the Grade 2 Unbridled Sydney Stakes in trademark fashion.

Her gate speed will undoubtedly be an asset in the King's Stand, while the choice of a stiff five furlongs with an uphill finish looks the right one for a mare who has always shown toughness at the end of five and a half.

As Qatar Racing's US adviser Fergus Galvin observed after the Shakertown: "I think that's her 12th or 13th win and she's never finished second. She knows where that winning post is."

Ascot will be new ground for Cox, who landed his first Breeders' Cup victory as recently as 2018 when Monomoy Girl took the Distaff but has already extended that number to eight, including four wins during the 2020 meeting at Keeneland.

Like his star mare, he knows where the winning post is.

## STAR RATING
★ ★ ★ ★

159

# Hong Kong in the hunt

SUCH is the eyewatering prize-money on offer in Hong Kong that it has been hard going for Ascot's international recruiters to gain traction with connections in the Asian powerhouse.

British-born trainer Richard Gibson was the last to try when saddling Gold-Fun to be a close second in the 2016 Diamond Jubilee Stakes, a project undoubtedly aided by the fact owner Pan Sutong has long had horses trained in Europe.

Earlier this year Hong Kong-based trainers emerged from a relative lull in their international ambitions – a trend undoubtedly reinforced by the Covid-19 pandemic – with Douglas Whyte breaking new ground in Qatar and a healthy five-strong team performing with credit in Dubai on World Cup night.

Royal Ascot is now back in focus for one of their top sprinters, who will bid to follow Cape Of Good Hope (2005 Golden Jubilee) and Little Bridge (2012 King's Stand) into the record books.

Wellington will be travelling for the first time

but the six-year-old has long looked a candidate for international honours, especially given that he has a Group 1 success at seven furlongs to go with a trio of top-level victories over six.

Gibson has targeted the Queen Elizabeth II Jubilee Stakes with Wellington, who has arguably been unlucky not to win even more top honours, given he was well towards the head of the market for the Hong Kong Sprint in 2021, only to be badly hampered when four horses came down on the home turn.

The son of All Too Hard made amends under Ryan Moore last December, enjoying clear sailing while odds-on favourite Lucky Sweynesse found all manner of trouble in running.

That made it two wins to one in favour of Wellington but Lucky Sweynesse has been untouchable at Sha Tin since the turn of the year, relegating Wellington to four placed efforts in as many meetings.

There is no shame in such a run of seconds and thirds, given that Lucky Sweynesse rose to joint-third in the

latest Longines World Rankings on a mark of 124; any horse who can even breathe the same air has to be taken seriously if adapting to the change of scenery.

**"Wellington will be travelling for the first time but the six-year-old has long looked a candidate for international honours"**

It remains to be seen whether Moore is available to resume the partnership but, even if his services are claimed elsewhere, the formerly French-based Gibson can potentially call on Christophe Soumillon – who rode Gold-Fun seven years ago – while Wellington's regular partner Alexis Badel was one of the best judges of pace in France before his permanent move to Hong Kong in 2020.

## STAR RATING

★★★★

# Va va voom

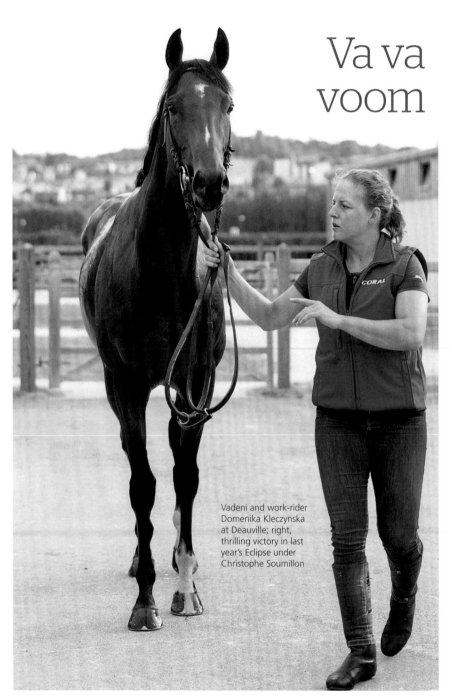

Vadeni and work-rider Domenika Kleczynska at Deauville; right, thrilling victory in last year's Eclipse under Christophe Soumillon

DESPITE having to wait deep into his career to taste success there, Jean-Claude Rouget has become quite adept at choosing which horses to send to the royal meeting.

In an era when the traditionally strong French challenge has been somewhat diminished, Rouget hit the target three times in as many years, with 2015 Coronation Stakes heroine Ervedya – whose son Erevann could be in line for a crack at the Queen Anne Stakes – and then Qemah, who won the 2016 Coronation and the 2017 Duke of Cambridge Stakes.

Since then Olmedo was a notable disappointment in the 2019 Queen Anne but Rouget is sufficiently sure in his own judgement not to embark on the trip unless he is confident of what he is travelling with.

There are few queries about either Vadeni's qualities or his ability to adapt to Britain, given his defeat of a galaxy of stars in last season's Eclipse, including Mishriff, Native Trail and an admittedly below-par Bay Bridge.

That performance gave an added international dimension to his stunning five-length victory four weeks earlier in the Prix du Jockey Club, a Classic which, in its modern form, is almost precision engineered to prevent wide-margin demolitions.

Victory in either the Irish Champion or the Arc might have meant we would not have seen Vadeni again except on the front of a stallion brochure.

But the Aga Khan's team and Rouget brought him back this year with two stated targets: the Prince of Wales's Stakes and, ultimately, an attempt at upgrading last year's runner-up effort at Longchamp on the first Sunday in October.

The son of Churchill ran a perfectly acceptable comeback to be fourth in a well-stacked Prix Ganay at the end of April, following the pattern of several of his trainer's high-profile horses when showing every sign that he was in need of the run.

Royal Ascot was always the aim for a peak performance and if the colt arrives there ready to explode in the way he did during midsummer in 2022, it will take a serious opponent to stop him.

Of course circumstances have dictated that the middle-distance division among the older horses is unusually deep, with horses such as Adayar, Desert Crown and Luxembourg also sticking around.

But Vadeni was champion three-year-old in Europe last year for a reason and, if Rouget decides his preparation has brought him to the boil, his presence in the line-up should be a huge hint.

## STAR RATING
★ ★ ★ ★ ★

# Record breaker gears up for big clash

**66**The key with Twilight Gleaming will be knowing when to light the fuse, since the stiff finish at Ascot could leave her vulnerable if she finds herself in front too soon**99**

THE chosen filly for Wesley Ward's favourite race at the royal meeting, Twilight Gleaming was run down late by Quick Suzy in the 2021 Queen Mary and returns two years later with something of a point to prove.

Like her former stablemate Campanelle, Twilight Gleaming is not a bulky US sprinter in the traditional sense, and was bred and bought in Europe.

However, where Campanelle was able to stretch out to six furlongs in the Commonwealth Cup at

that same 2021 meeting, this daughter of National Defense ideally wants the quickest ground and the shortest test that Ascot has to offer.

Having beaten the boys in the Grade 2 Breeders' Cup Juvenile Turf Sprint at the end of 2021, Twilight Gleaming could win at no higher than Listed level last term, failing to punch her ticket for a return to the Breeders' Cup when only fourth to Caravel in October.

That form turned out to be worth a whole lot more than anyone could have realised at the time and – on a weekend in April when record times were dropping like flies at Keeneland – she made a striking return to action when lowering the mark on turf for five and a half

furlongs under a motionless Irad Ortiz in the Giant's Causeway Stakes.

While Ward's two-year-olds are usually one of the great talking points of the build-up to Royal Ascot, he has proved on more than one occasion that he is more than capable of getting his horses to train on.

The key with Twilight Gleaming will be knowing when to light the fuse, since the stiff finish at Ascot could leave her vulnerable if she finds herself in front too soon.

In that context it was interesting to hear Ortiz say in his post-race comments at Keeneland that Ward had been working the filly from off the pace, and that he should feel free to ride her

however she felt comfortable.

Ward has a sole success in the King's Stand thanks to the remarkable Lady Aurelia in 2017, while whoever sends out the winner of the 2023 edition will almost certainly have got the better of a truly global array of sprinting talent.

The race promises Twilight Gleaming the chance of a rematch with Caravel, with the fastest two fillies in America facing fierce competition from Australia's sprint darling, Coolangatta.

With home stars Highfield Princess and Blue Azure also in the mix, what price there are no colts or geldings in the first five across the line?

## STAR RATING
★ ★ ★ ★

Twilight Gleaming
(6, centre) wins at the
2021 Breeders' Cup

# Is royal success written in the stars?

THERE wouldn't usually be too many Royal Ascot clues to be gleaned from the weekend action seven days after the Derby and just ten before the start of the meeting.

But Australian conditioning methods put a premium on backing up quickly, or else the use of barrier trials in the immediate run-up to a

target, and so few heads will have been turned down under when joint-trainer Troy Corstens announced that The Astrologist would have his final prep in the John of Gaunt Stakes over seven furlongs at Haydock.

That rethink came in the immediate wake of a British debut in the Duke of York Stakes that promised plenty

until the two-furlong marker, at which point the Zoustar gelding visibly tired.

Ryan Moore reported that he felt it had been a good run until The Astrologist blew up and that the outing would do him the power of good on the fitness front.

Such words from Britain's best must have reassured the Corstens camp given they

The Astrologist (12) goes close in the Al Quoz Sprint at Meydan

arrived at Marco Botti's Newmarket base off the back of arguably a career-best by The Astrologist when beaten a head by Danyah in the Group 1 Al Quoz Sprint at Meydan in March.

On that occasion Godolphin's Al Suhail and the Hong Kong pair Sight Success and Duke Wai were The Astrologist's nearest pursuers, giving the overall form an extremely solid look, however much of a surprise the identity of the winner might have been.

Having chased the pace, The Astrologist was passed by Al Suhail a furlong out but Damien Lane conjured a fine rally from him and the stiff six furlongs of the Queen Elizabeth II Jubilee Stakes looks tailor-made for the six-year-old.

He clearly thrives on being kept busy, since that run came off the back of sixth place in the Group 1 Newmarket Handicap and a flight from Melbourne to Dubai in the previous fortnight.

A tall, good-moving horse whose sheepskin noseband will make him easy to spot among the runners spread across the expanse of Ascot, he is easy to imagine travelling powerfully into the race and trading at much shorter than his starting odds.

It would also be no surprise to see him put in a powerful late burst; the question for backers will be whether he can live with the injection of pace from three to two furlongs out.

The key for his team is to ensure they put the necessary edge on him to stay in the fight when the speed is at its hottest.

## STAR RATING
★★★★

# Dangerous front-runner

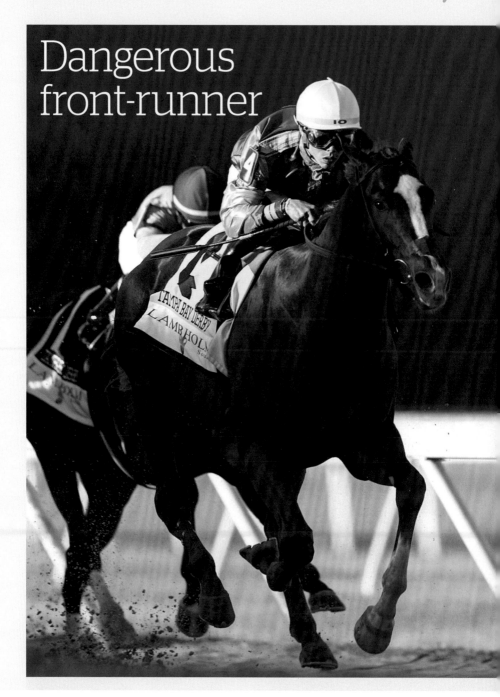

> **"If he has time to breathe on the front, he can be very tough to catch, as he showed in the Belmont Derby last year"**

KENNY McPEEK is something of a renaissance man among the ranks of US trainers, his tastes running the full gamut of challenges across the racing world.

With an increasingly rich American programme for middle-distance turf horses, it would be very easy to keep Classic Causeway at home and aim to build on his surprise debut on the surface last June, when an all-the-way success in the Belmont Derby accounted for Nations Pride and Stone Age.

But for a man who can tear himself away from Saratoga to visit the sales in Deauville every summer, and who is a frequent visitor to Tattersalls' Park Paddocks in Newmarket, the temptation to cast an eye across the Atlantic is never far away.

That Belmont success was only the colt's second start for McPeek after he was campaigned as a Kentucky Derby contender by previous handler Brian Lynch.

Nations Pride asserted superiority over the son of Giant's Causeway in the next two legs of the New York Racing Association's Turf Trinity series and McPeek even dabbled with a return to dirt at the start of this season, before pointing to the Arlington Stakes back on the turf of Churchill Downs as a final pre-departure prep.

A Racing Post Rating of 118 from that Belmont success suggests that, even in a year when the Prince of Wales's Stakes could be stacked with a clutch of Classic winners from the last two seasons, Classic Causeway's very best might put him in there pitching.

His trainer is keen to point out that a repeat of that mark or even better might well be contingent on being able to dictate the fractions from the front.

He told the Racing Post in May: "I think the turf is his preferred surface but equally he has to have the tactics his own way. If he has time to breathe on the front, he can be very tough to catch, as he showed in the Belmont Derby last year."

McPeek has enjoyed mixed fortunes with his racing raids in Europe. Hard Buck's runner-up effort in the 2004 King George has since been replaced in folk memory with Rosalind unshipping Kieren Fallon in the 2014 Coronation Stakes and Daddys Lil Darling bolting on the way to the start of the 2017 Oaks during the most theatrical of thunderstorms.

A change of luck would not be coming out of turn.

Classic Causeway: recast as a turf performer

## STAR RATING
★ ★ ★

Artorius: bids to improve on last year's close third in the Saturday sprint

# Ready to take closer order

IF EUROPEAN eyes have been accustomed to viewing Australian sprinters as one-dimensional – albeit highly effective – wrecking balls, then Artorius was something of a change of gear during a three-stop European campaign last summer.

Anthony and Sam Freedman undoubtedly hit on the perfect partner in Jamie Spencer for Artorius, a sprinter who rarely found his stride straight from the gates and was always doing his best work at the end of his races.

The uphill final drag at Ascot almost did the trick as Artorius – still a southern hemisphere three-year-old at the time – got to within three-quarters of a length of Naval Crown in the Platinum Jubilee.

He was third again in the July Cup, although this time his supporters never really got a proper shout as Alcohol Free had already well and truly flown by the time he got rolling.

A third trip to the well in the Prix Maurice de Gheest over an extra half a furlong proved too much of an ask but the Freedman team believe they are returning with enhanced prospects in 2023.

While sixth place in the Group 1 Newmarket Handicap was nothing to sneer at in March 2022, the son of Flying Artie has taken his form to a new level in the Australian autumn this year, landing a first Group 1 in the Canterbury Stakes at Randwick over six and a half furlongs before finishing just three-quarters of a length down on Anamoe, the country's best weight-for-age horse, over seven and a half in the George Ryder Stakes at Rosehill.

"I think he's definitely hitting Royal Ascot this year in better form than he was 12 months ago," said Sam Freedman. "He's not far off the likes of Anamoe and his win in the Canterbury has worked out, with the runner-up Imperatriz going on to win another Group 1.

"His form lines are strong and I think you guys will see a more tactically versatile horse. He'll be able to sit a lot closer, which will be important, whereas last year he was rattling home."

British and Irish punters who think they have the measure of Artorius going into the Queen Elizabeth II Jubilee Stakes may just want to take a second look.

Armed with some travellers' wisdom from their first adventure, the Artorius team have an upgrade on last year's performance firmly in mind.

## STAR RATING
★ ★ ★ ★

> **His form lines are strong and I think you guys will see a more tactically versatile horse. He'll be able to sit a lot closer, which will be important, whereas last year he was rattling home**

# Strength in depth

Other potential
contenders from
France and the US

FRENCH trainers could have a big say in the make-up of the Prince of Wales's Stakes, with the Wednesday feature boasting two more high-class entries in addition to Vadeni.

Fabrice Chappet's **Onesto** missed his intended comeback in the Prix Ganay because of the testing conditions and was then rerouted to the Prix d'Ispahan over 1m1f.

Equally adept at ten and 12 furlongs, the four-year-old's ideal scenario is fast ground and fast fractions to run at, a combination he may well get at Ascot.

Erevann: big chance
for France on day one

**Simca Mille** chased Onesto home in last year's Grand Prix de Paris and throughout his three-year-old season looked an out-and-out mile-and-a-half performer for Stephane Wattel.

But a comeback win in the Prix d'Harcourt and then a narrow defeat in the Ganay showed he is well up to Group 1 class back at the intermediate trip.

Last season's Prix Jean-Luc Lagardere winner **Belbek** looked in need of the run when third in the Prix Djebel, before a minor setback meant he missed the Poule d'Essai des Poulains (French 2,000 Guineas).

Andre Fabre is expecting to have the son of Showcasing back in full working order for the St James's Palace Stakes, a race the 31-time champion trainer has never won and which last fell to France with Sendawar in 1999.

Arguably the best chance of French success on day one could come in the Queen Anne Stakes with Jean-Claude Rouget's **Erevann**, who has only half a length to find with Inspiral on their meeting in last season's Prix Jacques le Marois, and who will have race fitness on his side.

Amo Racing have hit the woodwork on a number of occasions in the past couple of years at Royal Ascot and Kia Joorabchian might well be walking his box if their sizeable team have drawn a blank by Friday, when **New York Thunder** could be an intriguing candidate for the Commonwealth Cup for US trainer Jorge Delgado.

Unbeaten in a pair of starts at two, the son of Nyquist has some accomplished turf performers on the dam's side of his pedigree but will be coming off the back of a wide-margin Listed success on the Woodbine dirt in April.

Wesley Ward looks set to go for the King's Stand with **Love Reigns**, who was fourth in last year's Queen Mary and looked better than ever in her comeback success over five and a half furlongs at Keeneland in April.

# Powerful market force

**B**ROOME'S victory in the Hardwicke Stakes on the final day last year sealed an 11th leading trainer award for Aidan O'Brien and his first since 2019.

The Ballydoyle trainer sent out five winners last year, beating Godolphin's Charlie Appleby by one. The others were Little Big Bear (Windsor Castle Stakes), Kyprios (Gold Cup), Meditate (Albany Stakes) and Changingoftheguard (King Edward VII Stakes).

His total now stands at 81 winners and he is only one behind Sir Michael Stoute, the leading trainer at the meeting.

Three of last year's five winners – Little Big Bear, Kyprios and Changingoftheguard – were favourite (from seven market leaders in all). The other two were second favourite (Meditate) and third favourite (Broome) and the biggest-priced of the five was Broome at 6-1.

That reinforced the trend for O'Brien's best chances to be well indicated in the market. Sixteen of his 20 winners (80%) in the past five years were no bigger than 5-1 and nine went off favourite.

He has the occasional big-priced winner (most recently South Pacific at 22-1 in the King George V Handicap in 2019) and the best place to find one is in a race restricted to a single age group – two-year-olds or three-year-olds. All nine of his winners in the past decade priced in double figures fitted that criterion – three of those were ridden by Seamie Heffernan, so it is worth taking a look when he is on the second-string at Group 2 level and below.

Four of the nine came in juvenile races, including the Norfolk Stakes on two occasions (Waterloo Bridge at 12-1 and Sioux Nation at 14-1) when the winner was the stable's only representative and was ridden by Ryan Moore. O'Brien has had ten runners in the Norfolk in the past decade, mostly one a year, and apart from the two winners he has had a second, a third and three fourths.

Moore is worth noting when he has a handicap ride for O'Brien. The trainer has had three winners from 31 runners in that sphere since 2015 and it is notable that two were the only runners in their respective races and were ridden by Moore, returning SPs of 7-1 and 10-1. Moore had just 18 rides in handicaps for O'Brien in that timeframe, with four others finishing second at 7-1, 11-2, 4-1 and 2-1.

Another race where O'Brien could turn up a big-priced chance is the Jersey Stakes, with one of his three-year-olds who may not have made the top grade in miling or sprinting. From 16 runners in the past decade, he has had a winner (9-2), two

## 81
ROYAL ASCOT WINNERS

## 11
TOP TRAINER AWARDS

RACES OVER MIDDLE DISTANCES A STRONG POINT

**TOP TIPS**

FOCUS ON NORFOLK AND JERSEY RUNNERS

**1997**
YEAR OF FIRST
ROYAL ASCOT
WINNER

## O'BRIEN'S ROYAL ASCOT WINNERS BY AGE GROUP

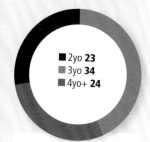

■ 2yo **23**
■ 3yo **34**
■ 4yo+ **24**

## MOST SUCCESSFUL RACES

Coventry Stakes
■■■■■■■■■

St James's Palace Stakes
■■■■■■■■

Gold Cup
■■■■■■■■

Queen's Vase
■■■■■■■

Chesham Stakes
■■■■■■

Hampton Court Stakes
■■■■

Hardwicke Stakes
■■■■

Prince of Wales's Stakes
■■■■

Queen Anne Stakes
■■■■

Coronation Stakes
■■■

Jersey Stakes
■■■

King Edward VII Stakes
■■■

Norfolk Stakes
■■■

Ribblesdale Stakes
■■■

Windsor Castle Stakes
■■■

seconds (one at 66-1) and two thirds (one at 14-1).

The Group races for middle-distance/staying types are a strong point. In the past decade he has had five winners in the Queen's Vase, three in the Ribblesdale Stakes and two apiece in the Hardwicke Stakes and King Edward VII Stakes. He had 14 runners-up in those four Group 2 races alone in the past decade, emphasising his competitiveness.

# Inspiral a team leader

THIS is the third Royal Ascot for the Gosden father-and-son team, who took the leading trainer award in 2021 with four winners but had a far less happy time last year.

There were ructions with jockey Frankie Dettori after he was beaten on Stradivarius in the Gold Cup and Saga in the Britannia Handicap in the space of a miserable hour on day three and they ended the meeting with just one winner from 30 runners.

That sole success came with 15-8 favourite Inspiral in the Coronation Stakes on day four, something of a redemption ride for Dettori after his travails the previous afternoon. The joint-trainers ended the meeting with the highest number of seconds and thirds (four of each), which illustrates their

## MOST SUCCESSFUL RACES

**Ribblesdale Stakes**
■■■■■
**Britannia Handicap**
■■■■
**Prince of Wales's Stakes**
■■■■
**Wolferton Stakes**
■■■■
**Chesham Stakes**
■■■
**Coronation Stakes**
■■■
**Duke of Cambridge Stakes**
■■■
**Gold Cup**
■■■
**King Edward VII Stakes**
■■■
**St James's Palace Stakes**
■■■

competitiveness amid the setbacks.

Overall the Gosden stable is second only to Aidan O'Brien at the past five meetings, with 17 winners to Ballydoyle's 20 in that time (next after the Gosdens is Charlie Appleby on 11).

Given that the Gosdens have plenty of runners, the key for punters is to find ways of narrowing the focus.

One angle is that the record with fancied runners is pretty good. In

the past decade, 18 of the Gosdens' 28 winners have been priced at 6-1 or below, from 69 runners in that category. The win percentage is 26%, although last year's difficulties sent them below the profit line.

It is worth noting that six of the other ten Gosden winners since 2013 were priced at 8-1 to 12-1 (and all in that price bracket were in the first six in the betting market), emphasising that it is rare for them to win with an outsider.

Handicap favourites are well worth watching, as two of the stable's four winners in that sphere in the past decade headed the market. The yard had 11 handicap favourites in that period, which works out at an 18% strike-rate (two others went close in second place).

Gosden snr has long been known for his patient handling of horses and it is often a good sign when the stable has a two-year-old ready to run at the meeting. From just 25 juvenile runners in the past decade, four won at odds of 7-4, 2-1, 10-1 and 20-1 (16%, +12.75pts).

PAY CLOSE ATTENTION TO RUNNERS AT 6-1 OR BELOW

**TOP TIPS**

LOOK OUT FOR TWO-YEAR-OLDS

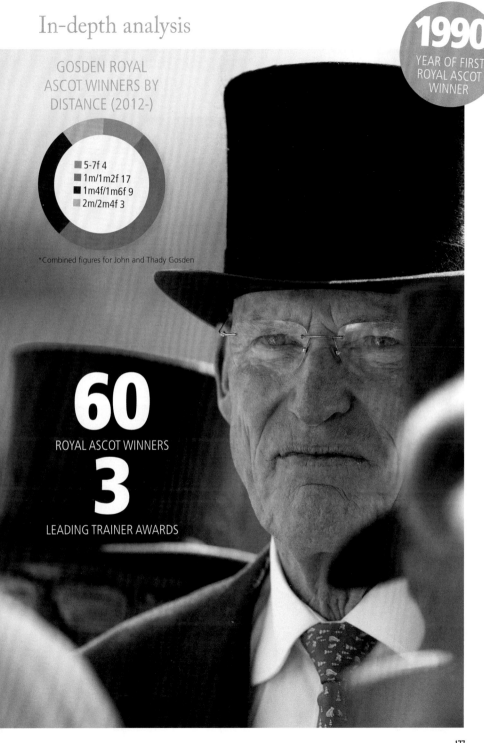

GOSDEN ROYAL
ASCOT WINNERS BY
DISTANCE (2012-)

- 5-7f 4
- 1m/1m2f 17
- 1m4f/1m6f 9
- 2m/2m4f 3

*Combined figures for John and Thady Gosden

**1990**
YEAR OF FIRST
ROYAL ASCOT
WINNER

**60**
ROYAL ASCOT WINNERS

**3**
LEADING TRAINER AWARDS

# Two-pronged attack

B OTH of the principal Godolphin trainers have been on the scoresheet in the past two years, bringing the operation's total to 14 at the past five Royal Ascots.

Eleven of the 14 were saddled by lead trainer Charlie Appleby, who provides the bulk of runners and winners nowadays, having taken his score to 15 in nine Royal Ascots since he stepped up from his previous job as assistant.

He has yet to take the

LOOK FOR LIGHTLY RACED 3YOS

**TOP TIPS**

HANDICAPPERS OFTEN SCORE AT GOOD ODDS

# In-depth analysis

leading trainer award but went close last year with a personal-best four wins, just one behind Aidan O'Brien. Two came in Group 1 races with Coroebus (St James's Palace Stakes) and Creative Force (Platinum Jubilee Stakes), taking his tally to five at the top level (along with Blue Point, 2018 and 2019 King's Stand Stakes, 2019 Diamond Jubilee Stakes). Clearly the big sprints are a strength.

Appleby's other two winners last year highlighted another key area: improving, lightly raced three-year-olds. Noble Truth (Jersey Stakes) and Secret State (King

George V Handicap) were both successful in races he had landed before in that category.

The Hampton Court Stakes, King Edward VII Stakes and Queen's Vase are other three-year-old races on Appleby's honours list. His winners of those races (along with the Jersey and King George V) came to Royal Ascot with an average of just over five runs (the highest number was eight) and notably all seven had won last time out.

Saeed bin Suroor, formerly the lead trainer and four times the award winner at Royal Ascot, is still capable of hitting the

target despite his reduced string.

Last year he struck with Dubai Future (20-1) in the Wolferton Stakes and his sole winner in 2021 was Real World (18-1) in the Royal Hunt Cup. Those winning odds perhaps illustrate that Bin Suroor's runners go under the radar nowadays.

His strength over the years has undoubtedly been older horses, with only three of his 38 winners coming in two-year-old races. A late developer in one of the handicaps or a Group 3 looks his most likely type now.

Handicaps can be a fruitful area in general for Godolphin runners, and the Royal Hunt Cup, King George V and Duke of Edinburgh are the three particularly worth focusing on. In the past decade, they have had eight winners from 57 runners in those three races (14%, +30.5pts). The winners came from five different trainers – Appleby, Bin Suroor, Roger Charlton, Mark Johnston and Mick Halford.

The other trainers who have got on the scoreboard under the blue banner in the past decade are Jim Bolger, Richard Fahey, Andre Fabre and Richard Hannon.

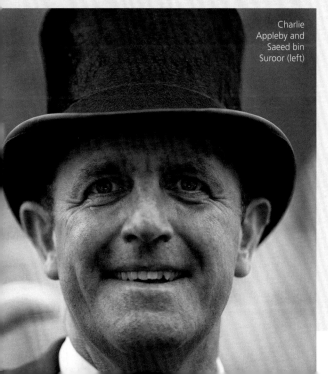

Charlie Appleby and Saeed bin Suroor (left)

# First knight

**S**IR MICHAEL STOUTE is clinging on as the leading all-time trainer at Royal Ascot with 82 winners after a blank last year saw his lead cut to just one by Aidan O'Brien.

That was only the ninth time Stoute had failed to score at the meeting since his breakthrough success with Etienne Gerard in the 1977 Jersey Stakes, five years after he had started training, and his record has been a model of consistency.

He retains a smattering of quality too, having had at least one Group 1 winner at the meeting in three of the last five years. He ranks sixth for Royal Ascot winners over that period with a total of seven.

Nowadays, though, he has come to rely on a handful of races for the bulk of his winners. The Hardwicke (eight), the Duke of Cambridge Stakes (five), the Duke of Edinburgh Handicap (four) and the King Edward VII Stakes (three) account for more than half of his winners since 2004 and they are likely to remain his strong points.

## MOST SUCCESSFUL RACES

**Hardwicke Stakes**
■■■■■■■■■■

**King Edward VII Stakes**
■■■■■■■

**Duke of Edinburgh Hcap**
■■■■■■

**Jersey Stakes**
■■■■■■

**King George V Handicap**
■■■■■

**Britannia Handicap**
■■■■

**Coronation Stakes**
■■■■

**Duke of Cambridge Stakes**
■■■■

**Prince of Wales's Stakes**
■■■■

**Queen's Vase**
■■■■

**Hampton Court Stakes**
■■■

**Queen Anne Stakes**
■■■

**Ribblesdale Stakes**
■■■

## STOUTE'S ROYAL ASCOT WINNERS BY DISTANCE 2009-

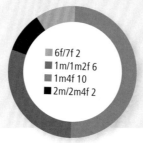

- 6f/7f 2
- 1m/1m2f 6
- 1m4f 10
- 2m/2m4f 2

## 82
ROYAL ASCOT WINNERS

## 6
LEADING TRAINER AWARDS

TAKE NOTE OF FILLIES BELOW GROUP 1 LEVEL

**TOP TIPS**

LOOK TO OLDER HORSES OVER 1M4F

What is notable about those favourite races is that three of the four are run at 1m4f. The exception is the Duke of Cambridge over a mile, although that race is for fillies and mares – a department where

**1977** YEAR OF FIRST ROYAL ASCOT WINNER

Stoute also tends to be well stocked.

Stoute's haul of 11 winners in the Hardwicke is the biggest number by any trainer in the modern era in a Group race at this meeting. He has also won the Duke of Edinburgh six times from not many runners since 1998.

Last year, from just eight runners, he went closest with Prince of Wales's runner-up Bay Bridge and had fourth places in the Wolferton, Royal Hunt Cup and Hardwicke.

Clearly he remains a force to be reckoned with, even if this turns out to be the year he is overhauled at the top of the Royal Ascot standings.

# First year in leading role

CHARLIE JOHNSTON goes it alone this year, having had his first Royal Ascot in 2022 as joint-trainer with father Mark. They drew a blank then and the task now is to re-establish the operation as the formidable force of old.

Mark Johnston ended his 35 years as a licence holder as the winningmost British trainer of all time and high on the list at Royal Ascot on 47 winners, with only Sir Michael Stoute, Aidan O'Brien and John (and Thady) Gosden ahead of him among current trainers.

Johnston snr remains full-time as assistant trainer and there is unlikely to be much variation in the modus operandi that served him so well.

The Middleham stable has had a dozen Royal Ascot winners over the past decade (last year was only the third blank in that period) and, true to form, most of them were in the longer-distance events.

Overall the score stands at six in the King George V Handicap (1m4f), undoubtedly one of Johnston snr's favourite targets, and there have also been multiple victories in the Queen's Vase (1m6f/2m, seven), Gold Cup (2m4f, four wins), Hardwicke Stakes (1m4f, four), Duke of Edinburgh Handicap (1m4f, four), King Edward VII Stakes (1m4f, three) and Queen Alexandra (2m6f, two).

Those seven races account for 64 per cent of the Johnston winners and the yard's runners are always worth a close look in the races where stamina and fitness are paramount. In the past decade, seven of the 12 Johnston winners have been at 1m4f-plus.

At the other end of the scale there have been two-year-old successes recently with Buratino (2015 Coventry Stakes), Main Edition (2018 Albany Stakes) and Raffle Prize (2019 Queen Mary Stakes).

Fancied juveniles are especially worth a close look. From 17 priced at 10-1 or below in the past decade, the stable has had two winners, two seconds and a third.

# Formidable competitor

IN JUST 14 years since his first Royal Ascot winner, US trainer Wesley Ward has established himself in the top ten current trainers at the meeting and as one of the most formidable competitors in sprint contests.

Since first taking the meeting by storm in 2009 with a pair of lightning-fast two-year-old winners in Jealous Again (Queen Mary Stakes) and Strike The Tiger (Windsor Castle Stakes), Ward has advanced his score to 12. He has had at least one winner at eight of the last ten meetings, missing out only in 2019 and last year.

Nine of those 12 wins have been over five furlongs, which suits his fast, precocious horses ideally. The other three have come with more mature runners, two over six furlongs and the other over a mile.

Ward has compiled that enviable record from only 83 runners, with his team each year typically numbering seven or eight. Last year he had five runners – his smallest number since 2013 – and they included Platinum

Jubilee Stakes third Campanelle and Queen Mary fourth Love Reigns. The big disappointment was Golden Pal, who was 15-8 favourite for the King's Stand Stakes but blew his chance with a slow start.

His 12 winners have come at a 14 per cent strike-rate with a level-stake profit of +32.5pts. The profit figure was skewed heavily by Strike The Tiger's 33-1 success in 2009 – before the threat posed by Ward's runners had been realised – and nine of his subsequent 11 winners have been no bigger than 13-2.

At odds below 7-1, Ward's strike-rate is 28 per cent (9-32) for a level-stake profit of 13.5pts, which demonstrates how well focused his team is on winning (five of the others were second).

The bulk of his runners and most of his winners have been in two-year-old races (8-60, 13%, +9pts).

# Scoreboard regulars

## ANDREW BALDING

The Kingsclere trainer is a growing force across the Flat season and has been on the Royal Ascot scoreboard in each of the last four years, taking his total to 11 winners. His sole winner last year was Coltrane in the Ascot Stakes, which was his third success in one of the meeting's heritage handicaps. He is strong across the board, with three winners at 2m-plus (including the Queen Alexandra Stakes twice) as well as three in juvenile events (Coventry, Albany and Windsor Castle Stakes). The market is a good indicator, with five of his eight winners at the last four meetings priced below 10-1 (15%).

## ROGER VARIAN

The Newmarket trainer moved into double figures at Royal Ascot last year when Eldar Eldarov (later the St Leger winner) landed the Queen's Vase. That made it eight winners at the last four meetings (three in 2019 and four in 2020) and it is notable that all of them were 8-1 or shorter and five (including Eldar Eldarov at 5-2) went off favourite. His record with favourites since 2019 is 1111210. Note his runners in the Hardwicke and Ribblesdale, plus handicaps such as the Buckingham Palace, Copper Horse, Palace of Holyroodhouse, Kensington Palace and Duke of Edinburgh.

## WILLIAM HAGGAS

The Newmarket trainer had the star of last year's meeting in Queen Anne Stakes winner Baaeed and added another success with Candleford in the Duke of Edinburgh Handicap, taking his Royal Ascot total to 14. Six have come at the last four meetings from 58 runners (10% strike-rate), along with six seconds, six thirds and seven fourths (43% in the first four). Conditions races below Group 1 over a mile and 1m2f have been a fruitful source in recent years.

## WILLIE MULLINS

The 17-time Irish champion jumps trainer got on the scoreboard again last year with Stratum in the Queen Alexandra Stakes, taking him to eight winners from 40 runners (20%) since his breakthrough in 2012. Last year's three runners finished first, second and fourth. All the wins have been in the Queen Alexandra Stakes and the Ascot Handicap and the strike-rate in those two races since 2012 is 28 per cent (+25.5pts). Six of the eight winners were ridden by Ryan Moore, although it is worth noting that Mullins used William Buick twice last year (including on Stratum).

## OTHERS TO NOTE

Northern-based **Richard Fahey** (two winners), **Karl Burke** (two) and **David O'Meara** (one) are regular scorers who got on the board last year. Fahey and Burke, in particular, do best at distances below a mile (accounting for eight of Fahey's ten winners and all five of Burke's), and **Kevin Ryan** is another northern trainer with a similar profile. Lambourn trainer **Clive Cox** (two winners from 47 runners at the past five meetings) continues to punch above his weight and five of his six winners in the past decade have come at 5f or 6f.
The big southern stables of **Charlie Hills** and **Richard Hannon** enjoyed more

Richard Fahey (inset) and Karl Burke

success last year and should be highly competitive again (Hannon also had three places last year), while fast-rising Newmarket trainer **George Boughey** was last year's breakout star with two winners.

At the past seven Royal Ascots, **Alan King** has had four winners from 27 runners (15%) plus two seconds, a third and two fourths. The strike-rate rises to 18 per cent at 1m4f-plus.

**Charlie Fellowes'** Newmarket yard has a notable strike-rate (three winners and four places from just 27 runners since 2018).

## LEADING ROYAL ASCOT TRAINERS IN THE LAST FIVE YEARS

| Trainer | Wins | 2nds | 3rds | Runs |
|---|---|---|---|---|
| Aidan O'Brien | 20 | 21 | 18 | 193 |
| John & Thady Gosden* | 17 | 12 | 14 | 139 |
| Charlie Appleby | 11 | 6 | 11 | 93 |
| Andrew Balding | 8 | 6 | 7 | 112 |
| Roger Varian | 8 | 5 | 7 | 78 |
| Sir Michael Stoute | 7 | 7 | 9 | 56 |
| William Haggas | 6 | 7 | 6 | 65 |
| Charlie (& Mark) Johnston* | 6 | 5 | 8 | 119 |
| Richard Fahey | 4 | 3 | 2 | 61 |
| Karl Burke | 4 | 0 | 1 | 33 |
| Willie Mullins | 3 | 4 | 2 | 21 |
| Wesley Ward | 3 | 4 | 2 | 36 |
| Charlie Hills | 3 | 4 | 1 | 47 |
| Charlie Fellowes | 3 | 2 | 2 | 27 |
| Alan King | 3 | 2 | 0 | 18 |
| Jessica Harrington | 3 | 1 | 2 | 22 |
| Kevin Ryan | 3 | 0 | 4 | 32 |

Includes trainers with at least three wins since 2018
*Includes joint and individual figures

# Frankie Dettori

# Last hurrah

ROYAL ASCOT 2023 will mark the end of an era as Frankie Dettori graces the meeting for the final time as part of his farewell tour before retirement at the end of the year. Any winner is sure to be celebrated with his trademark flying dismount and a tremendous ovation from the packed stands. It is going to be emotional.

Dettori will certainly be hoping it is a happier occasion than last year, when some lapses of judgement led to a public falling-out with long-time supporter John Gosden and left him with just one winner (Inspiral in the Coronation Stakes) from the five days.

It was a rare low point at the meeting. In the 33 years since his first success there in 1990 at the age of 19, Dettori has become the leading modern-day jockey at Royal Ascot with 77 winners and had only six blank years.

Having taken his number of leading jockey awards to seven with back-to-back titles in 2019 (seven winners) and 2020 (six), he has slipped back a little in the past couple of years but still three of his four winners in that time were in Group 1s.

He remains a man for the big occasion, with all bar two of his 21 winners in the past five years coming in Group 1 and 2 races (his last handicap winner was Persuasive in the 2016 Sandringham).

The Gosden stable again provided the majority of his rides last year (18 out of 22) and, with bridges swiftly mended after a

**TOP TIP**

BEST CHANCES WITH GOSDEN AND WARD RUNNERS

brief trial separation, that is likely to be the case again, although it would not be a surprise to see a wider clamour for his services at his retirement meeting.

The other mainstay for Dettori in recent years has been Wesley Ward, the US trainer for whom he has won Group 1 prizes in the Diamond Jubilee on Undrafted and the Commonwealth Cup on Campanelle, as well as the Queen Mary twice on flying juvenile fillies (Lady Aurelia in 2016 and Campanelle in 2020).

Watch out in particular when those top trainers turn to Dettori for their biggest rides. At the last seven royal meetings where Dettori has appeared (he missed 2017 with an arm injury), he has had 50 rides at 6-1 or less for Gosden/Ward and they have included 14 winners (28 per cent strike-rate) and six seconds.

The same is true when he is called up for a fancied runner from another stable. In the past seven years he has had 14 rides at 6-1 or less in Group 1/2 races for trainers other than Gosden and Ward and brought home four winners, two seconds and two thirds.

If there is one area where

punters should be wary, it is when Dettori rides a big handicap fancy. Almost inevitably these mounts are overbet and, while ten of his Royal Ascot winners have come in handicaps, he is showing a sizeable loss in recent years.

Many of his mounts may be overbet this year. Everyone remembers this is the course where he achieved his phenomenal Magnificent Seven in 1996 and memories are still fresh of the Royal Ascot day in 2019 when he threatened something similar by riding the first four winners on the card.

## MOST SUCCESSFUL RACES

**Gold Cup**
■■■■■■■■

**Ribblesdale Stakes**
■■■■■■■■

**Queen Anne Stakes**
■■■■■■■

**Chesham Stakes**
■■■■

**King Edward VII Stakes**
■■■■

**Norfolk Stakes**
■■■■

**Prince of Wales's Stakes**
■■■■

**Queen Mary Stakes**
■■■■

**St James's Palace Stakes**
■■■■

**Sandringham Handicap**
■■■

**1990**
YEAR OF FIRST ROYAL ASCOT WINNER

**77**
ROYAL ASCOT WINNERS

**7**
LEADING JOCKEY AWARDS

Having lit up Ascot and the racing world for the best part of 35 years, Dettori will be desperate for one final blaze of glory.

# Master at work

**B**Y ALMOST any measure Ryan Moore outstrips his rivals at Royal Ascot. In the past five years he has ridden 25 Royal Ascot winners – more than double the number of every jockey apart from Frankie Dettori and William Buick – and they have come in 18 different races. His versatility and tactical awareness are second to none.

Last year he took the leading rider award for the ninth time with seven winners, moving him to a total of 73 and only four behind Frankie Dettori in the list of current jockeys. Even if he does not surpass the soon-to-retire Dettori's total this year, he will take the mantle as the meeting's top rider by the time 2024 rolls around.

Moore's nine leading rider awards have come in 13 years since his first in 2010, having been backed first by Sir Michael Stoute and latterly by Aidan O'Brien. With the top two active trainers at Royal Ascot making him their main man, it is no surprise that his results are excellent year after year.

Moore's win tally in the

## MOST SUCCESSFUL RACES

**Hardwicke Stakes**
■ ■ ■ ■ ■ ■

**Chesham Stakes**
■ ■ ■ ■ ■

**Queen's Vase**
■ ■ ■ ■ ■

**Duke of Edinburgh H'cap**
■ ■ ■ ■

**Hampton Court Stakes**
■ ■ ■ ■

**Queen Alexandra Stakes**
■ ■ ■ ■

**Ascot Handicap**
■ ■ ■

**Britannia Handicap**
■ ■ ■

**Coventry Stakes**
■ ■ ■

**Gold Cup**
■ ■ ■

**King Edward VII Stakes**
■ ■ ■

**QEII Jubilee Stakes**
■ ■ ■

**Ribblesdale Stakes**
■ ■ ■

**Windsor Castle Stakes**
■ ■ ■

past five years is almost matched by his number of seconds (22), which is a sign that he regularly puts his mounts in a position to win. In that period 41 per cent of his mounts finished in the top three and 16 per cent were winners.

While punters can be confident Moore will give

them every chance if they back his mounts, he is not necessarily profitable from a betting perspective. Almost half of his winners in the past five years were favourite (12 out of 25), with only two returned at bigger than 7-1. His biggest-priced winner at Royal Ascot came last year in the Wokingham Handicap aboard 18-1 shot Rohaan.

That win came for David Evans and a possible tactic for punters would be to support Moore in lower-level races. Since 2012 he has had 56 'outside' rides (ie other than for O'Brien or Stoute) in non-Group races and 11 have won at an excellent strike-rate of 20 per cent. His record in that category last year was 2161, the other winner being Thesis at 14-1 in the Britannia Handicap for Harry and Roger Charlton.

Bookings for top jumps trainer Willie Mullins should be noted. In long-distance races their record is 6-16, 38%, +16.5pts.

Ryan Moore with trainer
David Evans after last
year's Wokingham win
on Rohaan (left)

**73**
ROYAL
ASCOT
WINNERS

**9**
LEADING
JOCKEY
AWARDS

# Elite level

**W**ILLIAM BUICK has been on the scoreboard at the royal meeting in all but one of the last 12 years (the blank came when he was missing in 2019 following a serious fall) and his record at the past five meetings (13 wins from 100 rides) is bettered only by Ryan Moore and Frankie Dettori, the top two active riders.

Eleven of his first 12 winners were for John Gosden but most since then have been in Godolphin blue (or associated colours) as their first jockey. Three of last year's five winners were for Godolphin lead trainer Charlie Appleby – Coroebus (St James's Palace Stakes), Secret State (King George V Handicap) and Noble Truth (Jersey Stakes).

Since 2015 Buick is 10-90 (11%) on Appleby runners, albeit at a small loss despite winners at 16-1 and 20-1.

It is interesting that six of Buick's 13 winners at his last four royal meetings came from 'outside' sources. Last year he won for Jane Chapple-Hyam (Saffron Beach in the Duke of Cambridge Stakes) and Willie Mullins (Stratum in the Queen Alexandra Stakes).

In other recent years he teamed up successfully with Marco Botti, Charlie Fellowes, David Menuisier and Ian Williams. Looking at that list, it is clear Buick's Newmarket connections serve him well.

His strike-rate since 2018 on non-Godolphin runners is 6-35 (17%) and the level-stake profit is huge at +76pts after Reshoun's victory at 66-1 for Wiliams in the 2021 Ascot Handicap.

As well as the occasional big-priced winner, Buick is pretty good at getting his fancied mounts in the shake-up. Last year he was in the first four on eight of the 15 priced below 10-1 and won on three of them for a small level-stake profit.